A Teacher's Guide to Coaching

Practical strategies for using coaching practices in schools

Jasmine Miller

Although every effort has been made to ensure that website addresses are correct at time of going to press, Hachette Learning cannot be held responsible for the content of any website mentioned in this book. It is sometimes possible to find a relocated web page by typing in the address of the home page for a website in the URL window of your browser.

Hachette UK's policy is to use papers that are natural, renewable and recyclable products and made from wood grown in well-managed forests and other controlled sources. The logging and manufacturing processes are expected to conform to the environmental regulations of the country of origin.

To order, please visit www.HachetteLearning.com or contact Customer Service at education@hachette.co.uk / +44 (0)1235 827827.

ISBN: 978 1 9152 6140 3

© Jasmine Miller 2025

First published in 2025 by
Hachette Learning,
An Hachette UK Company
Carmelite House
50 Victoria Embankment
London EC4Y 0DZ
www.HachetteLearning.com

The authorised representative in the EEA is Hachette Ireland, 8 Castlecourt Centre, Dublin 15, D15 XTP3, Ireland (email: info@hbgi.ie)

All rights reserved. Apart from any use permitted under UK copyright law, no part of this publication may be reproduced or transmitted in any form or by any means, electronic or mechanical, including photocopying and recording, or held within any information storage and retrieval system, without permission in writing from the publisher or under licence from the Copyright Licensing Agency Limited. Further details of such licences (for reprographic reproduction) may be obtained from the Copyright Licensing Agency Limited, www.cla.co.uk

Typeset in the UK.
Printed in the UK.
A catalogue record for this title is available from the British Library.

This book is dedicated to the teachers – those who inspire, nurture and empower with open minds and compassionate hearts. Your willingness to embrace new ideas, develop your skills, and adapt to the ever-changing needs of your students reflects your unwavering commitment to growth. These skills not only transform your classrooms but enrich all aspects of your life, strengthening relationships and fostering self-awareness. This book is also my way of giving back to our profession, honouring your dedication and supporting your journey. May it inspire you to continue leading with courage, curiosity and care. The world is brighter because of you.

Jasmine Miller is a teacher, a qualified and accredited coach and researcher. Her teaching career began in 2001 within primary mainstream schools in London before moving into special education and culminating in a decade of headship. Originally from New Zealand and now based in Scotland, she works globally with schools and other organisations who are interested in applying coaching practices and developing coaching cultures. Jasmine also divides her time as a CollectivED fellow with Leeds Beckett University, a research supervisor at the University of East London, and Non-Executive Director for bOunceT – a social enterprise supporting children and adults with disabilities. Her research includes coaching, neurodiversity and pupil voice. She is currently undergoing a PhD at the University of Stirling and has a master's degree in E-Inclusion, Learning Disability and Technology, and in educational research.

Reviews

Experienced coaches and newcomers alike will enjoy this accessible text, which is a welcome addition to the field of coaching in education. It is full of gems that spark interest, insights and reflections. I was absorbed while reading it from beginning to end, yet each chapter can comfortably stand alone, and readers can dip into individual chapters as required. The practical strategies for using coaching practices are thoughtfully and clearly described, and each chapter concludes with a summary and reflection questions, which can be used by the individual reader or as a focus for discussion in professional learning groups. The work is enhanced by the voices of educators who speak of their coaching experience with students, colleagues, direct reports and line managers. And of course, Jasmine's own reflections on coaching add a richness to the book. A valuable contribution to our work in education – and highly recommended!

Margaret Barr, coaching psychologist and former secondary headteacher

A Teacher's Guide to Coaching, by Jasmine Miller, is a timely and transformative resource for educators seeking to cultivate a coaching culture within their schools. As someone who has had the privilege of working alongside Jasmine as a fellow coach and trainer, I can attest to her deep understanding of both the art and science of coaching. This book is not just a guide, it's an invitation to rethink how we approach professional development and school improvement. Jasmine brilliantly outlines how coaching can empower teachers, students and entire school communities, fostering a culture of continuous growth and reflective practice. Her insights are grounded in real-world experience, offering practical strategies that are both actionable and impactful. In a time when schools need more than ever to support and inspire their staff, this book provides the roadmap. *A Teacher's Guide to Coaching* is a must-read for anyone committed to education.

Richard Reid, leadership coach and trainer

As a teacher and a coach in education, it is so refreshing to immerse in a book that is perfectly geared for the education setting, with a clear understanding of the needs of schools, teachers, leaders and students alike. Having worked with Jasmine, I can attest to her passion for quality education and her pure enjoyment when working with teachers and children.

A Teacher's Guide to Coaching is an invaluable resource for educators striving to unlock the full potential of their students and colleagues. It illuminates the transformative power of coaching, emphasising the integration of coaching principles into daily practices, and demonstrating how teachers and school leaders can foster an environment of growth, reflection and collaboration.*A Teacher's Guide to Coaching* puts the ball firmly in the court of everyone – making all stakeholders accountable for improving student outcomes through a coaching approach. However, it does this by empowering individuals – teachers and students alike – to set goals, navigate obstacles and realise their aspirations. Jasmine expertly outlines how adopting a coaching mindset can shift conversations from directive to empowering. Her work reminds us that when teachers model coaching behaviours, they inspire the same qualities in their learners. I will be recommending this in my colleagues' regular professional reading for sure.

Belinda Grieve, primary school teacher and former pedagogy coach

Contents

Foreword by Robin Macpherson 1

Acknowledgements 3

Introduction 5

Chapter 1   **Coaching: a journey through its origin and growth in education** 9

                The historical roots of coaching and the emergence of modern coaching 9

                The professionalisation and role of coaching in education 11

                Coaching and challenges in education 13

                The impact and future of coaching in education 15

                Coaching vs a coaching approach 17

                The promise of coaching in education 18

                Summary 19

                Reflection questions 20

Chapter 2   **Building a coaching culture: establishing the foundations for success** 21

                Foundational principles that underpin a coaching culture 22

                Leadership and buy-in 24

                Continuing professional development 25

                Introducing coaching in schools 26

                Addressing uncertainty and building acceptance 27

                Coaching infrastructure 29

                Sustaining momentum 30

                Summary 33

                Reflection questions 34

Chapter 3	Empowerment: the intersection of coaching and teacher agency	35
	Coaching and its role in education	36
	The power of ecological agency	36
	Coaching as a tool for empowerment	37
	What does empowerment through coaching look like?	37
	Designing coaching programmes for empowerment	40
	Summary	41
	Reflection questions	41
Chapter 4	Coaching competencies, frameworks and approaches: a personal exploration	43
	ICF core competencies and their relevance	43
	The EMCC and its competencies	44
	The Global Framework for Coaching and Mentoring in Education	46
	The GROW model	48
	The GROWTH model	52
	Clean Language and Clean Setup	57
	Integrating coaching models into practice	61
	Summary	62
	Reflection questions	63
Chapter 5	Coaching contracting: setting the stage for success	65
	The importance of establishing a coaching contract	65
	The chemistry session: finding the right fit	66
	Boundaries and expectations	67
	Work between sessions	68
	Summary	69
	Reflection questions	70

Chapter 6	Charting the path: visioning and goal setting in coaching 71
	The importance of visioning and goal setting 71
	The SMART goal-setting approach 73
	Summary 74
	Reflection questions 75
Chapter 7	Developing coaching skills: the art of connection, listening and powerful questioning in great coaching 77
	What makes a great coach? 77
	Underpinning coaching beliefs 78
	The power of active listening 79
	Powerful questioning 80
	Building rapport 81
	Staying in the not knowing 82
	Managing silence 83
	Summarising 84
	Paraphrasing 85
	Reflective practice 86
	Giving and receiving feedback 87
	Summary 89
	Reflection questions 90
Chapter 8	Time to think: the transformative power of reflection 91
	The elusive nature of time in schools 91
	The power of structured reflection 93
	Creating a thinking environment in the classroom 95
	The power of time to think 98
	Wellbeing through reflection 101
	Reflection as a catalyst for professional growth 104
	Building a reflective culture 105

	Summary	106
	Reflection questions	106
Chapter 9	**Emotional intelligence in coaching: the heart of the matter**	109
	The role of emotional intelligence in coaching	109
	Cultivating emotional intelligence as a coach	110
	The impact of emotional intelligence on the coaching relationship	116
	The transformative power of emotional intelligence	120
	Summary	121
	Reflection questions	121
Chapter 10	**Coaching skills for children and young people**	123
	Understanding the power of coaching for children and young people	123
	Building emotional intelligence through coaching	124
	Fostering independence and problem-solving	125
	Promoting positive communication skills	127
	Creating a coaching culture in schools	128
	Long-term benefits of coaching for young people	130
	Summary	131
	Reflection questions	131
Chapter 11	**Coaching skills for parents: empowering families in school communities**	133
	Building trust and bridging gaps	133
	Practical strategies for building parent partnerships through coaching	135
	The importance of coaching skills for parents and communities	138
	Summary	139
	Reflection questions	139

Chapter 12	**Coaching supervision for teachers who coach** 141	
	Enhancing coaching skills through supervision 141	
	Managing emotional and ethical complexities 143	
	Fostering continuous learning and professional growth.......... 144	
	Strengthening school coaching cultures through supervision...144	
	The essential role of supervision for teacher-coaches............. 145	
	Summary 146	
	Reflection questions..147	
Chapter 13	**Changes to teaching approaches through coaching: the voices of teachers**.. 149	
	Evolving relationships within the school community 151	
	Summary..153	
	Reflection questions... 154	
Chapter 14	**Equality of relationships: transforming school dynamics through coaching** 155	
	The shift from hierarchical to collaborative relationships.........155	
	Enhanced interpersonal dynamics.................................... 156	
	Empowerment through voice...157	
	Promotion of mutual respect... 158	
	Supporting organisational change 160	
	Summary..162	
	Reflection questions.. 163	
Chapter 15	**Transferable skills: beyond the classroom** 165	
	Enhanced communication skills.. 165	
	Refined questioning techniques 167	
	Increased self-awareness... 168	
	Impact on professional relationships 169	
	Contribution to a supportive educational environment............170	

	Summary	171
	Reflection questions	172
Chapter 16	**Next steps: bringing coaching into your practice**	173
	Practical tools you can use right away	175
	Moving forward	177
	Your next steps	177
	Stay connected and continue learning	179
	Further resources for coaching in education	179
Bibliography		180

Foreword

A few years ago, I was looking for someone to help me set up some professional learning about coaching. I needed a skilled and experienced practitioner to work with staff at the school I had just started at, and I especially needed someone experienced that I could trust. This was proving to be a challenge; finding people who understand coaching in the business world isn't hard, but I firmly believe that coaching in education is much more nuanced and needs someone who fundamentally understands the complexity and challenge of school life. I reached out to my network and eventually got a very strong recommendation about someone called Jasmine Miller. I managed to get in touch with her and asked if she would be able to meet me. In a moment of quite remarkable serendipity, it turned out that Jasmine lived a five-minute walk from my house, so we agreed to meet for a coffee. It was the beginning of one of the most inspiring and beneficial friendships I've ever had.

Since that day, Jasmine has worked with staff in two different schools for me and has also worked with a group of parents. The feedback has always been superb, and for many reasons. She has an incredible depth of knowledge about education, based on her experience of working in several schools in different contexts. It was this experience that developed her professional curiosity about coaching, and her extensive reading and research has made her one of the most informed voices on how it can be harnessed in educational settings to improve outcomes for all. She is also one of the most emotionally intelligent people you could ever want to meet, and this comes through in every chapter. When she told me that she was writing this book I was delighted, because it is going to do a power of good in the world of education.

Coaching has been one of the most positive developments that I've seen in my time as a teacher and school leader, but there is still a long way to go before it is systematically embedded. Like many others, I have personally benefited from training to be a coach, and being coached myself, as a part of my leadership development. However, coaching has broader application than just leadership, and this book explores a fantastic range of possibilities for multiple stakeholders, so it should be read by everyone with a vested interest in education. One of the hardest things to do is to embed coaching across a whole school, but this book gives important guidance on how this can be done. I'm particularly keen that we use coaching with children as another important tool in the pastoral toolkit, because this helps them to achieve agency, which Jasmine explores in chapter 10.

What makes this book stand out is the extent to which it is rooted in evidence. Jasmine is as well versed as anyone I know in coaching research and she has used this knowledge to cover a wide range of applications and approaches. She is also a very clear communicator, so the text isn't weighed down in technical jargon and impenetrable analysis; it is definitely a book by a teacher, for teachers, with very practical application. The different models, approaches and ways in which coaching can be used to build a school's culture are all explored fully and with refreshing clarity.

Coaching is a substantial professional skill set, and it takes a lot of time and practice to get to a basic level of competence. There are many people out there who claim that they can provide training in this, but very few of them have actually worked in education. Jasmine has extensive experience as a teacher and school leader, so this book really is your best bet at becoming a proficient coach. It's not something that happens overnight and it takes a lot of personal reflection, but the juice is definitely worth the squeeze.

So, as you work your way through this book, get ready to expand your thinking and make sure you share what you learn. Coaching is about building relationships and sharing great practice, so you are about to embark on a very rewarding journey. Enjoy!

Robin Macpherson
Teacher and author

Acknowledgements

I want to extend my heartfelt gratitude to all the teachers who have generously shared their experiences, reflections and stories about coaching. Your insights have been invaluable, and they continue to inspire others in the coaching community to grow and develop. I look forward to staying connected as we continue on this journey together.

A special thank you to John Feltham (former headteacher at Woodlands School, Harrow), Catherine Corrie (author of *Becoming Emotionally Intelligent*), Kim Morgan (CEO of Barefoot Coaching), Margaret Barr (Margaret Barr Coaching Psychology and Hypnotherapy), Professor Rachel Lofthouse (professor of teacher education at Carnegie School of Education, Leeds Beckett University), Robin Macpherson (head of Robert Gordon's College), Professor Christian Van Nieuwerburgh (global director, Growth Coaching International), Chris Munro (executive director, Growth Coaching International), Richard Reid (leadership coach and trainer) and Nicole Osborne (marketing manager) for their wisdom, guidance and support throughout my journey.

I want to express my deepest gratitude to my husband, Geoff, for his unwavering support. Your belief in me, your encouragement and your willingness to listen to all of my ideas, no matter how big or small, have been invaluable. You have been my rock through every challenge and triumph, always standing by my side with love, patience and understanding. I could not have achieved what I have without you, and for that I am forever grateful. Thank you for being my constant source of strength and inspiration.

Introduction

The idea for this book comes straight from my heart, inspired by my own journey as a teacher, school leader and professionally accredited coach. I have been fortunate to work alongside some incredible educators and, through those experiences, I have come to see just how powerful coaching can be in our profession. My aim here is simple: I want to share these insights with you and create a space where we can explore how coaching can truly enrich our teaching practices.

This book is not just a guide; it is a collection of voices, thoughts and experiences from teachers like you. Written for teachers, by a teacher, it is all about how coaching can be woven into the fabric of our classrooms to support both our personal growth and professional development. Sprinkled throughout the book, you'll find the reflections and insights of the teachers I spoke to during my journey. Their stories bring the ideas in these chapters to life, offering real-world examples of how coaching has transformed their teaching practices, relationships with students and interactions with colleagues. These reflections highlight the impact of coaching on their day-to-day experiences and provide you with relatable perspectives on how these coaching principles can be applied in your own context. Through their voices, you will gain a deeper understanding of the practical benefits of coaching and how it can enrich not just your professional life but your personal growth as well.

The focus of this book is on the broadly facilitative approach to coaching, which sits near the non-directive end of the coaching continuum. This approach emphasises reflection, self-discovery, and empowering the coachee to find their own solutions, aligning with a belief in the potential of individuals to grow from within. While this book explores facilitative coaching in depth, it is important to note that instructional coaching, which takes a more directive stance, is another highly valuable approach, especially when educators need more specific, actionable guidance. For those interested in instructional coaching, I recommend exploring the work of Jim Knight, whose books and resources are available at www.instructionalcoaching.com.

Coaching is a practice that anyone can begin using, however I also believe in the importance of professional coaching training. Whether you are just starting or have already embraced coaching in your school, investing in accredited training can provide you with the deeper knowledge, skills and confidence to coach more effectively. Professional training equips you with tools to navigate complex situations, offers ethical guidance and builds a solid foundation in the core competencies of coaching, ensuring that you approach coaching conversations with clarity and impact. If you ever have the opportunity to seek out such training, I encourage you to consider it as a valuable investment in both your career and the lives of those you coach.

By diving into these pages and trying out some of the ideas shared, you'll have the chance to:

- get to know yourself better, both as an educator and as a person
- build stronger relationships with your students, colleagues and families through effective coaching practices
- add new tools to your teaching toolkit to engage and inspire young minds using coaching techniques
- learn how to bring coaching into your classroom, school and beyond, shaping a culture that thrives on support and growth.

Each chapter of this book is designed to be practical and reflective. At the end of every chapter, you'll find a summary along with reflection questions to help you process what you've learned and think about how it applies to your own context.

When I spoke to teachers about what they wanted from a book on coaching, their responses were clear:

- practical tools they could use right away
- ways to truly listen and connect with what someone is saying
- techniques to break free from fixed ways of thinking
- strategies to help students overcome their fear of failure
- guidance on when, how and whether a coaching approach is right for the classroom
- ideas for using coaching with younger children
- approaches to be less judgemental and more supportive when helping others.

To address these needs, I've structured the book around some key aspects of coaching in schools. I've always believed that teaching is about so much more than delivering content; it's about creating connections, fostering growth and nurturing potential. In the fast-paced, ever-changing environment of a school, it can be easy to lose sight of the small, transformative moments that happen every day. Coaching offers a way to slow down, reflect and be more intentional in how we approach those moments – both for our students and for ourselves.

Through the stories and strategies shared in this book, I hope you'll find a renewed sense of purpose and possibility. Whether you are new to coaching or have been using it for years, there is always something more to discover. Coaching isn't a one-size-fits-all approach; it is a flexible, evolving practice that can be adapted to suit your unique context and the diverse needs of your students.

This book is a starting point; the real work happens in your classrooms, staffrooms and communities. As you read, experiment and reflect, I encourage you to make this journey your own. Take what resonates, adapt what needs adjusting and, most importantly, keep the conversation going – with yourself, your colleagues and your students.

Thank you for picking up this book and for your commitment to your own growth as an educator. I am excited to see where coaching takes you and your school community. And as you embark on this journey, remember that you are not alone – we are all in this together, learning, growing and making a difference, one conversation at a time.

Reflection questions

Before you jump in, I invite you to reflect on a few things:

1. What have your experiences been like with coaching, both giving and receiving?
2. How would you describe coaching in your own words?
3. What changes do you see in others when you use coaching?
4. What do you notice about yourself when you engage in coaching?
5. What else would you like to gain from reading this book?

Chapter 1
Coaching: a journey through its origin and growth in education

The historical roots of coaching and the emergence of modern coaching

The historical roots of coaching stretch back much further than we might initially assume, embedded within humanity's long-standing pursuit of self-betterment, wisdom and growth. As social beings, humans have always sought guidance from one another, whether through mentorship, philosophical discourse or leadership. Coaching, in its various forms, reflects this deep-seated human need for connection and support in navigating the complexities of life. From the dialogues of ancient philosophers like Socrates, whose method of questioning encouraged deep reflection and self-discovery, to modern practices, coaching has evolved in response to the cultural, political and social needs of each era.

In its modern sense, coaching began to take shape in the latter half of the twentieth century, particularly with the groundbreaking work of Tim Gallwey in the 1970s. Gallwey's *The Inner Game of Tennis* (1974) represented a shift in how we think about learning and performance. His core insight – that the greatest obstacles to success are often internal rather than external – challenged traditional methods of instruction, which tended to focus on correcting errors and imparting expertise. Gallwey's approach, instead, emphasised the importance of self-awareness, mental clarity and the removal of internal barriers to performance.

This was a significant departure from the hierarchical, teacher-centred models of learning that had dominated educational and professional development contexts. Gallwey's work suggested that true progress and learning occur when individuals are supported in cultivating their own self-knowledge, in line with the belief that the most profound change comes from within. By encouraging individuals to become more attuned to their internal experiences – thoughts, feelings and beliefs – coaching became more about guiding individuals towards their own solutions rather than providing prescriptive advice.

The influence of Gallwey's 'Inner Game' philosophy reached far beyond sports, permeating fields such as business, personal development and, crucially, education. His ideas resonated with a growing recognition that the psychological aspects of performance – confidence, motivation, mindset – were just as important as technical skills or knowledge. This perspective laid the foundation for many of today's coaching practices, which prioritise personal reflection, goal setting and the removal of internal blocks to success. However, it is important to recognise that the development of coaching was not isolated to Gallwey's work. The emergence of coaching as we understand it today was shaped by several intersecting trends throughout the twentieth century. The rise of humanistic psychology, with figures like Carl Rogers, introduced concepts such as unconditional positive regard, active listening and non-directive guidance, all of which have become integral to the coaching relationship. Rogers' client-centred therapy emphasised the importance of creating a safe and empathetic environment in which individuals can explore their thoughts and feelings without judgement – principles that deeply influenced coaching's emphasis on co-creating a trusting, open relationship between coach and coachee.

As society shifted towards greater individualism in the late twentieth century, especially in Western contexts, the idea of self-improvement and personal mastery gained traction. This societal shift, combined with the growing professionalisation of coaching, led to the establishment of coaching as a formal practice with defined methodologies, frameworks and ethics. Professional coaching organisations such as the International Coaching Federation (ICF) and the European Mentoring and Coaching Council (EMCC) emerged in the 1990s, providing accreditation and defining core competencies for coaches. This professionalisation brought coaching into the mainstream, and solidified its role in personal and professional development across industries.

In educational settings, coaching has found a particularly important role. Teachers, like athletes or business professionals, benefit from a reflective process that helps them improve their practice, not by merely focusing on external standards or performance metrics, but by fostering deeper self-awareness and intentionality in their work. The practice of educational coaching has been shown to enhance teaching effectiveness, improve classroom management and foster a more collaborative school culture, benefiting both educators and students. By helping teachers reflect on their practice, set meaningful goals and navigate challenges, coaching fosters a culture of continuous learning and improvement in schools.

This historical evolution of coaching reveals how it has consistently adapted to meet the changing needs of individuals and societies. From its roots in mentorship and philosophical inquiry to its modern incarnation as a structured, reflective practice, coaching has always been about more than simply imparting knowledge. It is about creating the conditions for personal and professional growth, empowering individuals to tap into their potential and navigate the complexities of their lives with greater clarity and purpose.

As you read through this chapter and the ones that follow, I encourage you to think about how coaching could fit into your school's culture. How can you create the conditions for learning and growth? How can coaching help you, your colleagues and your students reach their full potential? These are the questions that lie at the heart of this book, and I am excited to explore the options with you.

The professionalisation and role of coaching in education

The professionalisation of coaching in education is a critical step in solidifying its role as a transformative practice. Although there remains no single, universally accepted definition of coaching, it is now widely recognised as a process that enhances self-awareness, facilitates goal setting and fosters accountability (van Nieuwerburgh, 2012; Whitmore, 2017). This structured yet flexible approach allows individuals to explore their potential and identify the internal and external factors that influence their growth. Within educational contexts, coaching is uniquely positioned to empower teachers and students alike, creating opportunities for deeper reflection, improved performance and a more engaged learning environment.

Coaching's integration into schools has been particularly significant because it taps into the evolving understanding of education as more than just the transmission of knowledge. The traditional view of education, which often focused solely on content mastery and performance outcomes, has given way to a more holistic understanding of the learning process. This shift emphasises the development of personal and professional capacities – such as adaptability, resilience and relational skills – that are critical to both teaching and learning in the modern world.

One of the key insights in understanding the role of coaching in education is the recognition that the personal characteristics of teachers can greatly influence how they enact their professional agency. In other words, it is not just about what teachers know; it is about who they are and how they continuously grow and adapt in their roles. Coaching creates the space for this type of reflective growth, offering teachers the opportunity to examine their beliefs, values and teaching practices in a supportive environment. This reflective process enables teachers to develop a deeper sense of self-awareness, which in turn influences their professional practice and interactions with students and colleagues.

The impact of coaching on teacher agency is particularly profound. According to Priestley, Biesta and Robinson (2015), teacher agency is not a fixed characteristic but a dynamic process shaped by the individual's capacity to reflect on and respond to the ever-changing demands of their professional environment. Coaching helps teachers build this capacity by encouraging critical reflection and supporting them in navigating the complexities of their work. In doing so, it not only enhances their ability to respond to challenges but also empowers them to take ownership of their professional development, aligning with the broader educational goals of empowerment, engagement and lifelong learning.

Coaching in schools is not just a trend or a passing initiative – it is a transformative practice that has the potential to reshape the educational landscape. As schools increasingly recognise the importance of fostering environments where teachers feel supported and empowered, coaching becomes an essential tool for creating a culture of continuous learning. This culture is one where professional development is not simply a one-time event or a box to be ticked but an ongoing process that helps educators refine their practice, build resilience and inspire others.

At its core, coaching encourages teachers to model the same reflective, growth-oriented behaviours they seek to instil in their students. In this way, coaching promotes a more engaged, dynamic learning environment where both teachers and students are active participants in the learning process. The ripple effect of coaching is profound – when teachers feel empowered and supported, they are better equipped to inspire, challenge and nurture their students, ultimately leading to improved student outcomes.

The professionalisation of coaching has provided educators with a framework that emphasises the importance of self-awareness, goal setting and personal growth. It recognises that teachers are not merely transmitters of knowledge but individuals who must continuously evolve in response to the changing demands of their profession. By creating a space for reflection, dialogue and accountability, coaching fosters a deeper sense of professional agency and engagement, empowering teachers to take charge of their growth while aligning with the long-term goals of educational transformation.

Coaching in education is far more than a tool for improving classroom practice. It is a dynamic, transformative process that encourages educators to engage in lifelong learning, develop their professional agency and inspire positive change within their schools. As research continues to explore the impact of coaching in education, it is becoming increasingly clear that its benefits extend far beyond individual teacher development, contributing to the creation of more engaged, reflective and resilient school communities.

Coaching and challenges in education

Coaching in education is a deeply transformative process, focused on creating environments where both learning and personal growth can thrive. As John Whitmore emphasises, 'Coaching is not teaching at all; it is about creating the conditions for learning and growing' (Whitmore, 2017, p. 6). This reframing of the teacher's role – from imparting knowledge to nurturing a student's capacity to engage in self-directed learning – broadens our approach to education, and highlights the teacher's role in nurturing flexible learners and independent thinkers. Coaching moves beyond the traditional classroom dynamic and creates space for both teachers and students to unlock their potential, fostering a culture of continuous growth within the school community.

Over the years, a variety of coaching models have been developed to guide educational practice, each offering a structured yet flexible approach to implementing coaching. From Egan's three-stage model (Egan, 2002), which focuses on exploring current situations, setting goals and taking action, to the GROW model (Goal, Reality, Options, Will) (Whitmore, 2009) and the OSCAR (Outcome, Situation, Choices, Actions, Review) framework (Gilbert and Whittleworth, 2009), these models offer a systematic way of embedding coaching into daily interactions. Despite their differences, they share a common emphasis on fostering reflection, facilitating self-directed learning, and supporting growth through questioning, active listening and appropriate challenge.

In educational settings, these models are not just theoretical tools but practical frameworks that can help teachers and students navigate the complexities of learning and development. The GROW model, for instance, is widely used in schools as it helps both teachers and students set clear goals, reflect on their current realities, explore various options and commit to actions that will move them towards their desired outcomes. This structured approach encourages a reflective mindset, helping educators to continuously adapt and refine their teaching practices while empowering students to take ownership of their learning.

Yet, while coaching offers many benefits, it is not without its challenges. One of the most significant issues cited in the literature is the conceptual ambiguity surrounding coaching, particularly the lack of a standardised legal definition (van Nieuwerburgh, 2017). This ambiguity can lead to varied interpretations of what coaching actually entails, which, in turn, affects its implementation in schools. Some educators may view coaching as a directive process, akin to mentoring, while others see it as a non-directive form of support aimed at fostering self-reflection and personal growth. This lack of a clear definition can create confusion, both in terms of how coaching is delivered and how its success is measured.

The ambiguity surrounding coaching can make it difficult to gain buy-in from all stakeholders in a school community. Teachers, senior leaders and even students may have different expectations of what coaching should look like, which can lead to inconsistent application across different contexts. For coaching to have a lasting impact, it requires not only a shared understanding of its purpose but also a commitment from everyone involved to engage fully in the process. Without this alignment, coaching risks being perceived as just another educational trend, rather than the transformative practice it has the potential to be.

Despite these challenges, the core purpose of coaching in education remains clear: to help individuals realise their potential by fostering self-belief and self-awareness. This aligns with Maslow's Hierarchy of Needs (1943), where self-actualisation – the realisation of one's full potential – is the ultimate goal of personal development. Coaching plays a crucial role in this process by creating the conditions in which individuals feel safe to reflect on their strengths and areas for growth, explore new possibilities and take meaningful steps towards achieving their goals.

The connection between coaching and self-actualisation becomes especially important in educational settings. Students and teachers alike benefit from environments that prioritise not just academic achievement but personal growth and wellbeing. When coaching is integrated into the fabric of school culture, it provides a supportive framework that encourages individuals to move beyond self-limiting beliefs, explore their aspirations, and develop the skills and confidence necessary to achieve their goals. For students, this might mean taking ownership of their learning journey, while for teachers, it could involve reflecting on their teaching practices and seeking new ways to inspire and engage their students.

The journey to self-actualisation, both for students and educators, is not a straightforward one. Coaching, by its very nature, involves navigating uncertainty, discomfort and challenge. As teachers and students confront the internal and external barriers that stand in their way, the coaching process provides a supportive space for reflection, exploration and growth. This can be a deeply rewarding experience, and it also requires a willingness to engage with vulnerability and change.

In practice, one of the key challenges in coaching is ensuring that it is delivered in a way that is sensitive to the diverse needs of individuals within a school community. No two teachers or students are the same, and coaching must be tailored to reflect these differences. This requires coaches to be not only skilled in the use of coaching models and techniques but also attuned to the emotional, cultural and social contexts in which their coachees operate. The ability to adapt coaching approaches to meet the unique needs of individuals is critical to ensuring that coaching has a lasting, positive impact.

Despite the challenges, coaching offers a powerful tool for transforming educational environments. When coaching is embedded within school culture, it fosters a space where learning can flourish, empowering individuals to take ownership of their personal and professional development and, ultimately, contributing to a more engaged and resilient school community.

The impact and future of coaching in education

The impact of coaching in education is increasingly evident, as more schools recognise its potential to enhance both teaching and learning by fostering self-directed growth. Research consistently highlights the positive outcomes of coaching, particularly in areas such as staff performance improvement, enhanced wellbeing and the support of continuous professional development (Gore, 2014; Adams, 2016; Lofthouse, 2019a). Additionally, coaching serves as a vital conduit for peer support among educators, creating opportunities for collaboration, shared learning and mutual growth (Jewett and McFee, 2012; Lofthouse and Hall, 2014).

However, despite this growing acknowledgement, coaching has not yet been fully embedded as a cultural norm within the United Kingdom's educational system. While there are schools and educators who have embraced coaching, it remains an underutilised tool for many. Peter Hawkins (2012) describes a coaching culture as one in which coaching is central to how leaders, staff and even students engage and develop, enhancing organisational performance and fostering a more resilient, adaptive community (p. 21). Achieving such a culture, however, demands more than simply implementing coaching programmes on an ad hoc basis – it requires a fundamental shift in how schools approach professional development, leadership and teacher support.

The establishment of a coaching culture in schools is a multifaceted process that requires dedication and alignment at every level of the organisation. It begins with a commitment to viewing coaching not as a one-off intervention but as a continuous and integral part of the school's growth. This may involve embedding coaching into leadership development programmes, where school leaders not only model coaching practices themselves but also encourage the use of coaching in their teams. Similarly, coaching techniques can be woven into staff meetings, professional development sessions and even classroom observations, ensuring that reflective dialogue and goal setting become regular features of school life.

Peer coaching among teachers represents another powerful avenue for embedding a coaching culture. When teachers engage in coaching relationships with their colleagues, they create a supportive space for sharing expertise, reflecting on challenges and exploring innovative practices. This type of collaboration fosters a sense of collective responsibility for student outcomes and professional development, breaking down the silos that often exist in educational environments. Peer coaching also empowers teachers to take ownership of their growth, encouraging a shift away from top-down models of professional development towards a more distributed, collaborative approach.

For coaching to become truly embedded in the fabric of schools, it must extend beyond formal coaching sessions. The goal is to create an environment where coaching principles – such as active listening, reflective questioning and solution-focused thinking – are naturally integrated into everyday interactions. This could mean that a school leader adopts a coaching approach when discussing challenges with a staff member, or that teachers apply coaching techniques when working with students to foster independence and self-awareness.

The future of coaching in education lies in this broader, more holistic use of coaching principles. It requires a shift in mindset, where coaching is not viewed as an additional task but as an essential part of how schools function and grow. With the right support, training and leadership, schools can cultivate a culture where coaching is a natural and integral part of their approach to professional development, leadership and student success.

In this coaching-centric culture, the potential benefits are vast. Teachers are empowered to take control of their professional journeys, students develop greater self-awareness and ownership of their learning, and school leaders foster an environment of continuous improvement. As research and practice continue to evolve, the impact of coaching in education is likely to become even more pronounced, shaping the future of learning in ways that promote resilience, collaboration and sustained growth for all members of the school community.

Coaching vs a coaching approach

While coaching and a coaching approach share foundational principles, they serve distinct purposes and are applied differently in various contexts. Coaching refers to a formal, structured relationship where a trained coach works one to one or with a group to help the coachee(s) set specific goals, overcome challenges and achieve personal or professional growth. This process typically involves dedicated time for deep exploration, goal setting and reflection, often using frameworks like GROW or GROWTH (Goals, Reality, Options, Will, Tactics and Habits) (van Nieuwerburgh, 2020) to guide the conversation. Coaching sessions are intentional and focused on measurable outcomes, with the coach acting as a facilitator rather than a directive expert. The transformative nature of formal coaching lies in its ability to provide the coachee with a safe, non-judgemental space to reflect, gain clarity and build a strategy for change, often leading to significant shifts in mindset, behaviour and performance over time.

In contrast, a coaching approach is less formal and more fluid, integrating the core principles of coaching, such as active listening, powerful questioning and fostering self-reflection, into everyday interactions. The key to a successful coaching approach lies in your way of being as a coach or educator. This refers to the attitude, presence and mindset you bring to every interaction, whether it is with a student, a colleague or a parent. A coaching approach is most effective when it is rooted in a way of being that is open, non-judgemental and curious, creating a safe space where others feel empowered to explore their own solutions.

For instance, a teacher might use a coaching approach with a student who is finding a project difficult. Instead of offering direct solutions, the teacher might say, 'What ideas have you thought about so far, and how do you think they might work?' This approach allows the student to engage in critical thinking and problem-solving, and what makes it truly powerful is the teacher's way of being. If the teacher asks the question with genuine curiosity, patience and a belief in the student's ability to find their own answers, the impact is far greater. The student feels supported, heard and trusted, which encourages them to take ownership of their learning. The teacher's way of being, calm, open and trusting has created the conditions for deeper reflection and growth.

While formal coaching is typically more intensive and focused on achieving specific outcomes, a coaching approach creates a culture of continuous development and self-directed growth. By integrating a coaching way of being into everyday interactions, educators and leaders encourage individuals to think critically, take responsibility for their learning, and engage in meaningful conversations that empower rather than direct. This shift in mindset helps build resilience, independence and a growth-oriented environment where everyone feels valued and capable. Both formal coaching and a coaching approach can drive positive change. Coaching tends to foster deep, focused transformation, and a coaching approach sustains a growth mindset, collaboration and problem-solving in day-to-day interactions, making it accessible and impactful across multiple contexts.

The promise of coaching in education

As we explore the origins and growth of coaching in education, it is clear that coaching offers a powerful means of fostering personal and professional growth. However, its success depends on how it is implemented and the context in which it is used. My hope is that this book will provide you with the insights, tools and inspiration you need to integrate coaching into your own practice, helping to create a learning environment where both teachers and students can thrive.

As we journey through the chapters, remember that coaching is more than just a set of techniques or practices – it is a way of being. It is about how we approach our work, our relationships and our own development. It's about fostering a mindset that values reflection, growth and continuous learning. And most importantly, it's about creating a supportive environment where everyone can succeed. Let's embark on this journey together and see how we can bring the transformative power of coaching into our schools, classrooms and lives.

Summary

- Coaching has evolved from its philosophical roots to formalisation through organisations like the ICF and EMCC.
- The use of coaching promotes self-directed growth, improves teacher performance and enhances collaboration in schools.
- Coaching models, such as the GROW and OSCAR frameworks, are practical applications for using coaching in education.
- Challenges in coaching include conceptual ambiguity and inconsistent implementation, limiting wider adoption.
- The distinction between coaching and using a coaching approach makes coaching more accessible and impactful.
- Embedding coaching principles into everyday school practices is key to creating a sustainable coaching culture.
- Coaching practices can reshape educational environments, fostering continuous growth and collaboration among teachers and students.

Reflection questions

1. How do you currently view the role of coaching in education?
2. What aspects of coaching and a coaching approach resonate most with your personal approach to teaching and professional development?
3. How could coaching be used to enhance the culture and practices in your school or classroom?
4. What challenges might you face in implementing coaching practices in your educational setting, and how could these be addressed?
5. Reflect on a time when you were coached or acted as a coach. What impact did that experience have on your growth or the growth of others?

Chapter 2
Building a coaching culture: establishing the foundations for success

Creating a successful coaching culture within an educational setting is about fundamentally rethinking how growth, development and leadership are approached within the school environment. A coaching culture is one where the principles of coaching are embedded into the fabric of the organisation, influencing everything from how teachers interact with students to how leaders support their staff. It represents a shift from traditional top-down management styles to a more collaborative, reflective and growth-oriented approach.

In this chapter, we will explore the essential elements needed to establish a robust coaching culture in schools. We will delve into the foundational principles that underpin a coaching culture, the importance of leadership buy-in, and the role of continuous professional development. Building a coaching culture is not a one-time effort but an ongoing commitment to fostering an environment where everyone, from students to senior leaders, is encouraged and supported to reach their full potential. I will share some insights from teachers about their experiences of coaching being introduced in their schools. A coaching culture does not emerge overnight; it requires careful planning, intentional actions and a shared vision that aligns with the school's broader educational goals. As we explore these concepts, you will gain insights into the practical steps needed to lay the groundwork for a coaching culture that is not only sustainable but also transformative. This chapter offers you information and tools to help you begin your journey towards creating a school environment where coaching is more than just a practice; it is a way of being.

What exactly is a coaching culture? It can be described as an environment where coaching principles and practices are seamlessly integrated into the daily life of the school. It's more than just having a few coaches on staff or offering occasional coaching sessions. A true coaching culture is one where everyone, from the leadership team to classroom teachers, sees coaching as a valuable and integral part of their professional growth. In a coaching culture, conversations take on a deeper, more reflective nature, focused on personal and collective growth. People feel empowered to engage in open, honest dialogue about their goals, challenges and areas for development. Feedback isn't something to be feared; it is embraced as a tool for growth, always delivered with the intent to help someone improve. Everyone in the school community is committed to continuous development, not just for themselves but for their colleagues and, most importantly, for their students.

Foundational principles that underpin a coaching culture

At the heart of any successful coaching culture are foundational principles that help transform the entire environment into one that nurtures growth and potential. When I think about what makes coaching truly impactful, it is the shift in mindset that moves away from telling people what to do, to creating the conditions where they can discover their own path.

One of the first principles is trust and psychological safety. Without this, nothing else can really flourish. Trust is what allows people to feel vulnerable enough to engage in honest conversations. When we coach, we're not just asking people to think about their actions; we are asking them to reflect deeply on their motivations, their fears, their dreams. For this kind of exploration to happen, there needs to be a foundation of safety, people need to know that it is okay to take risks and make mistakes. This trust is not built overnight, but through consistent respect and understanding.

Equally important is active listening. Coaching isn't about jumping in with solutions or advice. It is about listening, really listening, not just to the words but to the emotions and intentions behind them. I have learned that when I listen deeply, I am able to ask better questions, ones that spark insight in the person I am coaching. Active listening shows that you value the other person's perspective, and that can be transformative. It is amazing how often we find that when someone feels truly heard, they can find the answers they were searching for themselves.

Then there is reflective practice, a cornerstone of any coaching relationship. Reflection allows people to step back and see the bigger picture. In schools, we are often so busy running from one task to the next that we forget to take a moment to reflect on what we've learned. I believe that coaching creates that space, a moment of pause where teachers and students alike can consider not just what they are doing, but why. Reflective practice doesn't just promote awareness; it builds self-awareness, which is the foundation of all growth.

Ownership and empowerment are equally important. One of the things I love most about coaching is how it encourages people to take responsibility for their own development. It is not about telling them what to do or prescribing a path; it is about helping them recognise their own strengths and capacity for growth. When someone realises that they hold the power to make changes in their own life, the shift is profound. They stop waiting for someone else to 'fix' things and start taking charge.

Closely linked to this is goal setting and accountability. Coaching helps people clarify their goals, whether personal, professional or academic. But it is not just about setting the goals; it is about holding themselves accountable for the steps they take towards achieving them. I have found that when individuals have someone who supports them through this process, who checks in and helps them stay on track, they are far more likely to follow through and succeed.

In coaching, non-directive support is another essential principle. This one can be tricky because, as educators, we are so used to offering solutions. But coaching asks us to resist that temptation. Instead, we guide individuals towards finding their own solutions. We ask questions that open up new ways of thinking and challenge assumptions. This respect for their autonomy, their ability to problem-solve, is powerful. It builds confidence, resilience and a deeper understanding that the real breakthroughs come from within.

Finally, a true coaching culture thrives on collaboration and shared learning. Coaching should not happen in isolation. When schools embrace coaching, it becomes part of the fabric of the community, fostering a culture where feedback and reflection are normalised. Teachers support one another, not just through structured coaching sessions but also through everyday interactions. Peer coaching, for example, creates an atmosphere where everyone learns from one another, and growth becomes a collective effort.

These principles – trust, active listening, reflection, empowerment, goal setting, non-directive support and collaboration – are the foundation of a coaching culture that can transform schools, businesses and even personal relationships. When these principles are woven into the fabric of a school, the impact is profound. It is not just about improving performance; it is about fostering environments where everyone feels valued, supported and capable of reaching their full potential.

Leadership and buy-in

For a coaching culture to truly set in, one of the most critical factors is leadership buy-in. Without the commitment and support of school leaders, coaching can quickly become just another initiative that is talked about but never fully embraced. Leadership sets the tone for everything, and if leaders don't champion coaching, it risks being seen as optional or peripheral rather than central to a school's growth and development. When leaders actively participate in coaching, whether through their own personal development or by embedding coaching practices into their leadership style, it sends a powerful message. It shows that coaching is not just for teachers or students but for everyone. Leaders who model coaching behaviours, like active listening, reflective questioning and encouraging autonomy, demonstrate the value of coaching in everyday interactions. This visible commitment from the leadership team helps build trust and credibility around the practice, making it more likely that teachers and staff will engage with coaching themselves.

Practical strategies

- Dedicate sufficient time and resources to coaching initiatives, positioning coaching as an integral and indispensable element of professional practice rather than an optional or luxury addition.
- Create space in the schedule for regular coaching conversations, making it a priority within the school's operations.
- Provide access to trained coaches for both staff and leadership, to ensure quality coaching experiences.
- Integrate coaching into professional development plans, embedding it within the broader strategy for staff growth and school improvement.
- Embed coaching into the school culture, weaving it into meetings, staff development sessions and everyday practices to make it a fundamental part of the school's DNA.
- Leadership buy-in should ensure coaching is central to the school's development strategy and seen as a critical tool for continuous improvement.

Leadership is also key to removing barriers to coaching. In some schools, coaching can be viewed with scepticism or even resistance, especially if teachers feel it's being imposed on them or see it as a tool for performance management rather than growth. Leaders play a vital role in addressing these concerns, creating a culture where coaching is framed as a supportive, non-judgemental process aimed at enhancing everyone's potential. Clear communication from leaders about the purpose of coaching that is focused on growth, not evaluation, helps to alleviate fears and build buy-in from staff.

Continuing professional development

Once there is a strong foundation for coaching, continuing professional development (CPD) becomes the fuel that keeps the momentum going. Coaching itself is a form of CPD, but it must be integrated into a broader professional learning framework to be sustainable and impactful. CPD ensures that coaching does not become a one-off initiative, but rather an ongoing process of learning, reflection and growth. In education, professional development is often thought of as attending workshops or training days, but coaching transforms CPD into something far more dynamic. Through regular coaching conversations, teachers have the chance to reflect on their practices, identify areas for improvement and set meaningful goals, all of which are directly tied to their day-to-day experiences in the classroom. This ongoing reflection is much more powerful than occasional training sessions because it is personalised and immediately applicable.

Coaching also encourages self-directed learning, a critical component of effective CPD. Rather than passively receiving information from external sources, teachers in a coaching culture take ownership of their development. They identify the skills and knowledge they want to build, reflect on their progress, and seek out the resources and support they need. This sense of autonomy and responsibility not only makes professional development more relevant and impactful but also instils a mindset of lifelong learning. When educators are continually growing, they become more resilient, adaptable and innovative. They develop qualities that are essential in today's rapidly changing educational landscape.

Furthermore, the impact of coaching on CPD extends beyond individual development. As teachers engage in coaching, they contribute to a culture of collaborative learning. Peer coaching, for example, provides opportunities for educators to learn from one another's experiences, share best practices and offer constructive feedback. This collaboration enhances the collective knowledge of the school and builds a community where continuous improvement is the norm. Schools with a strong coaching culture see professional development as a shared responsibility, where all – leaders, teachers and staff – support everyone else's growth.

In this way, coaching and continuing professional development are deeply interconnected. Coaching provides the structure and support for sustained, reflective learning, while CPD offers the broader framework for ongoing growth and improvement. Together, they form a powerful combination that not only enhances individual performance but also strengthens the entire school community. When the leadership team champions this approach and invests in creating a coaching culture, the result is an environment where both teachers and students can thrive, constantly evolving and adapting to meet new challenges.

Introducing coaching in schools

Introducing a coaching culture in schools often triggers natural human responses to change, particularly when it is implemented without sufficient context or explanation. Psychologists refer to this as the 'fear of the unknown', an instinctive reaction that prompts caution in unfamiliar situations. Doherty and Horne (2002) describe change as inherently disruptive, defining it as 'a difference, a variation, or a substitution of one state for another... becoming or making different'. In the fast-paced, ever-evolving environment of schools, these feelings of uncertainty can be amplified, especially when educators feel unprepared or unsupported. Resistance to change is often tied to our innate desire for control. Griffin and Tyrrell (2015) point out that humans prefer to remain in their comfort zones because that is where they feel safe and in control. When initiatives like coaching are introduced without careful planning and communication they can disturb this sense of stability, leading to anxiety, stress and scepticism. Michael Fullan (2001) highlights what he calls the 'implementation dip' – a period where things often get worse before they improve, as schools navigate the challenges of adopting new practices. During this initial phase, many educators may view coaching as just another passing trend rather than a meaningful, long-term change. This reflects the initial reactions I encountered when introducing coaching in schools.

Recognising the critical role of effective change management in one of my leadership roles, I decided to pursue a postgraduate certificate in coaching through Barefoot Coaching Ltd and Chester University. This training gave me a much deeper understanding of the knowledge and skills required to facilitate meaningful change within educational teams. One of the key insights I gained came from Robinson (2018, p. 86) who emphasises that coaches must engage with, rather than bypass, the underlying theories of action they wish to influence. Theories of action refer to the implicit or explicit beliefs, assumptions, and strategies that guide individuals' decisions and behaviours. These frameworks shape how people approach challenges, interpret situations, and respond to change. Understanding and addressing these theories of action is essential because they often underpin resistance or openness to new ideas. This concept highlighted for me the importance of not only identifying these implicit frameworks but also working collaboratively to address and refine them. It reinforced the critical role of aligning theory with practice in a way that resonates with the individuals involved, ensuring that any change introduced feels both purposeful and practical. By engaging deeply with these theories of action, coaches can create a shared sense of ownership and direction, making the process of change more meaningful, sustainable, and rooted in the realities of those it seeks to impact.'

A critical question emerged throughout my training: what kind of environment is needed for coaching to successfully foster learning and growth? This question became central to my reflection and practice as I worked to develop coaching approaches that could be applied effectively in educational settings. I realised that for coaching to truly thrive, it requires a supportive environment where open communication, trust and psychological safety are prioritised. When educators feel that their needs and concerns are being acknowledged, they are much more likely to embrace coaching as a valuable tool for personal and professional growth rather than see it as something to fear. This journey taught me that successful implementation of coaching in schools is about more than introducing a new practice; it is about creating the right conditions for change. By engaging educators in a thoughtful, well-communicated process, schools can navigate the initial discomfort and build a coaching culture that empowers everyone to learn, grow and thrive.

Addressing uncertainty and building acceptance

How do we go about addressing the natural uncertainty that change brings, especially when teachers feel unprepared or uninformed about what coaching really entails? Transparency is key, and clear communication is essential to help staff understand what coaching is, why it is being introduced and how it can benefit them. Think of it as providing a map before embarking on a journey – it won't remove all the obstacles, but it gives everyone a sense of direction. Priestley et al. (2015) emphasise the importance of providing support and clarity when introducing any new initiative. Without this, it is like asking someone to dive into a pool without telling them how deep the water is. By offering clear expectations and explaining the benefits of coaching, school leaders can help ease the discomfort that often accompanies change. Understanding how people adapt to change is key to addressing resistance and building acceptance. Several psychological models offer valuable insights:

- Intentional Change Theory (Boyatzis et al., 2013) highlights the importance of personal goals. If teachers see coaching as a way to achieve their own professional aspirations, they are more likely to engage with it.
- The Kübler-Ross Change Curve (Kübler-Ross, 1997) illustrates that adapting to change is not linear – people may move back and forth between stages of acceptance. This helps us understand why some teachers might embrace coaching quickly while others may need more time and support.
- Preston (2009) notes that change becomes harder to navigate as we get older, not because we are incapable of it, but because our comfort zones solidify over time. Recognising this helps us tailor coaching approaches to individual readiness, offering different levels of support as needed.

Coaching also plays a key role in fostering ecological agency, a concept that connects teachers' professional growth with their aspirations for their students' progress and wellbeing (Lasky, 2005). Effective change can occur only when teachers are actively involved from the start. Bakkenes et al. (2010) and Fullan (2007) highlight the importance of involving educators in shaping their own learning experiences.

One of the senior leaders who spoke to me when I was researching this book shared his reflections on two approaches to introducing coaching in his schools:

1. The first approach allowed teachers to choose their own professional learning paths, linking coaching to their specific needs and goals. This approach gave teachers autonomy, which enhanced their motivation to engage.
2. The second approach made coaching mandatory for all staff, embedding it into the school's policy. New staff received structured, intensive coaching training, ensuring clarity and consistency in the school's approach to professional development.

Both approaches show that, whether through personalisation or structure, creating an environment where teachers have some degree of ownership over their coaching experience is essential for success.

One of the biggest challenges schools face when introducing coaching is the pervasive culture of performativity, where teachers are often under pressure to meet targets, deliver quick results or prepare for inspections like Ofsted (Office for Standards in Education, Children's Services and Skills). Priestley (2015) reminds us that the structures and cultures of schools play a huge role in shaping teacher capacity. Coaching can offer a counterbalance to this performance-driven environment by promoting long-term growth and self-regulation. However, as Lofthouse (2015, 2016, 2018a) has noted, coaching initiatives can sometimes be sidelined by immediate pressures. Another teacher shared their experience of how coaching was deprioritised during an impending Ofsted inspection, despite its potential to foster real development:

'We knew we had an Ofsted inspection on the horizon, so all our energy went into that, and other areas of innovation were pushed to the side.'

Coaching can only flourish if it's protected from these external pressures. School leaders need to ensure that coaching is seen not as a distraction from performance but as a tool that enhances it over time.

Coaching infrastructure

For coaching to thrive, it must be thoughtfully integrated into the school's wider professional development framework. This involves strategic planning, ongoing support and the creation of reflective spaces where teachers can engage in meaningful discussions about their practice. Time and space for coaching conversations should be prioritised rather than squeezed in around other responsibilities. Once leadership support and staff buy-in are in place, the next step is to establish the infrastructure that will support coaching.

Practical strategies

- Identify and build on existing strengths within the school community, particularly focusing on strong relationships, to create a solid foundation for coaching.
- Encourage curiosity in staff and leaders to help them engage with coaching from a place of genuine interest in their own personal growth and in building relationships with others.
- Ensure that while coaching training may be mandatory, formal coaching conversations remain voluntary, allowing teachers to engage willingly for more impactful outcomes.

By engaging those who are genuinely interested in self-development, schools can foster a coaching movement that values openness, respect and active listening. Even in environments where time is scarce, creating moments for reflection is essential. Such spaces not only improve performance but also model the values that coaching seeks to instil: thoughtfulness, care and a willingness to listen.

Time is perhaps the most critical resource for successful coaching. It cannot be rushed or squeezed into an already packed schedule. Leaders need to rethink how time is allocated within the school day.

> **Practical strategies**
> - Set aside regular time slots for coaching conversations, or provide release time for teachers involved in coaching, whether as coaches or coachees.
> - Ensure the availability of the right physical or virtual spaces for coaching, offering privacy and comfort to signal that coaching is a serious, valued activity.
> - Establish clear processes and protocols to support coaching, including systems for:
>   - matching coaches with coachees
>   - tracking progress
>   - ensuring confidentiality.
> - Provide ongoing supervision and support for coaches, to help them refine their skills and maintain effectiveness.

When schools prioritise coaching and build the necessary infrastructure, the ripple effects are profound. A single coach can make a significant impact, but when a small group of motivated individuals commit to coaching, the benefits extend to the entire school community, teachers, support staff and, most importantly, the students.

Sustaining momentum

A key strategy for sustaining momentum is regularly celebrating and sharing the successes that coaching brings. When staff can see the tangible benefits of coaching, whether in improved teaching practices, better student outcomes or enhanced personal wellbeing, they are far more likely to stay engaged. This can be done by sharing case studies or testimonials from staff who have experienced meaningful growth through coaching. Showcasing real examples of how coaching has positively impacted the school helps to reinforce its value. Recognising and rewarding those who are championing coaching within the school, whether through formal recognition or informal praise, further strengthens commitment.

In my experience, when teachers hear first-hand from their colleagues about the benefits of coaching, it creates a ripple effect. Seeing how coaching has led to breakthroughs, whether in classroom management, lesson delivery or even personal wellbeing, inspires others to engage. It also helps to dispel any lingering doubts or scepticism about the effectiveness of coaching. Moreover, celebrating success doesn't just motivate individuals; it fosters a collective sense of progress, reinforcing the idea that the school is moving forward as one.

Another critical aspect of sustaining momentum is ensuring that the coaching process remains dynamic and responsive to the evolving needs of the school community. Coaching frameworks should not be static; they need to be regularly reviewed and updated to reflect new insights, challenges and goals.

Practical strategies

- Introduce new coaching models or techniques to keep the coaching process fresh and dynamic.
- Offer ongoing professional development for coaches, to help them stay sharp, inspired and aligned with emerging trends and priorities.
- Adjust the focus of coaching conversations to align with evolving school priorities, such as new curriculum initiatives or student wellbeing concerns.
- Ensure coaching frameworks are flexible enough to adapt to changes, keeping the practice relevant and meaningful for both teachers and students.
- Provide regular opportunities for coach development to bring in fresh perspectives that can reinvigorate coaching relationships.
- Keep coaching personalised and tailored to the specific needs of individual teachers, recognising that one size does not fit all in teacher development.
- Ensure the coaching process remains engaging and adaptable, avoiding routine and continuing to provide meaningful value for the school community.

Sustaining a coaching culture also requires embedding coaching into the everyday fabric of school life. It can't be something that happens in isolation; it needs to be woven into the broader goals and initiatives of the school.

The more deeply coaching is connected to the school's strategic priorities, the more likely it is to be sustained long-term. For instance, linking coaching to the school's goals around teacher wellbeing, professional growth and collaborative relationships can create a strong foundation for its continued relevance.

Coaching works best when it is aligned with the school's broader initiatives, whether these are to do with student wellbeing, curriculum development or performance management. The key is to show how coaching contributes to these priorities. For example, if the school is focusing on improving student outcomes, coaching could be framed as a tool for helping teachers refine their teaching practice.

If student wellbeing is the focus, coaching could be linked to helping staff build better relationships with students or manage their own wellbeing more effectively, so they are better equipped to support their students. In schools where performance management is a central concern, coaching can be positioned as a method for empowering teachers to meet their professional goals in a way that promotes self-reflection and growth, rather than just compliance. By integrating coaching into the existing structures and priorities of the school, it stops being an isolated initiative and instead becomes part of the everyday rhythm of school life.

Practical strategies

Supporting teacher wellbeing

- Integrate coaching as part of a wellbeing strategy to address teacher stress and burnout.
- Provide a supportive space for reflection, problem-solving and self-care through coaching conversations.
- Emphasise coaching as a tool for emotional and mental support, helping teachers thrive in demanding environments.
- Signal to staff that their personal health and professional growth are valued, fostering a more resilient teaching community.

Enhancing professional growth

- Use coaching to promote continuous learning by encouraging reflection on current practices and identifying areas for improvement.
- Help teachers set and achieve professional goals through guided coaching sessions.
- Keep teachers engaged by aligning coaching with lifelong learning, avoiding stagnation and motivating ongoing professional development.
- Integrate coaching with other professional development opportunities, creating a cohesive growth pathway beyond traditional training days or reviews.

> **Fostering collaborative relationships**
> - Leverage coaching to foster open communication, mutual respect and trust among teachers, students and parents.
> - Encourage coaching as a shared practice, strengthening relationships across the school community.
> - Use coaching not only for individual growth but to promote collective progress, contributing to a healthier and more collaborative school culture.

Ultimately, sustaining a coaching culture requires long-term vision and commitment from leadership. It is about creating a school environment where coaching isn't a one-time initiative but an ongoing process of reflection, growth and learning. This involves building a culture where coaching is valued, celebrated and embedded into every layer of school life. Through clear communication and ongoing support, and by linking coaching to the school's core values, objectives and strategic priorities, schools can create a sustainable coaching culture that continues to evolve and inspire both staff and students over time.

Summary

- The chapter examines the introduction and sustainability of a coaching culture in schools, focusing on addressing resistance to change.
- Transparency, leadership buy-in and clear communication are identified as key factors in overcoming resistance and supporting coaching initiatives.
- Psychological models are explored as tools to help navigate the emotional challenges of change in educational environments.
- Teacher involvement in the coaching process is emphasised as crucial for successful implementation and engagement.
- Coaching can be used as a method to counteract performativity pressures, support teacher wellbeing, enhance professional growth and encourage collaboration.
- Sustaining coaching momentum requires celebrating successes, keeping coaching relevant and aligning it with the school's strategic goals.
- Building a strong coaching infrastructure, including time, space and resources, is highlighted as essential for making coaching an integral part of daily school life.

Reflection questions

1. How can you, as a leader or educator, model the behaviours that support a coaching culture in your school?

2. How can you apply the concept of transparency in your own context to ease the introduction of coaching or other new initiatives?

3. What steps can be taken to ensure that time and space are allocated effectively for coaching in your school's schedule?

4. How can you keep the momentum for coaching going in your school over the long term?

5. Reflect on your current school culture. How close is it to being a true coaching culture, and what steps could be taken to move closer to that vision?

Chapter 3
Empowerment: the intersection of coaching and teacher agency

Through coaching, educators can experience a powerful sense of personal empowerment and self-discovery, as if a door to new possibilities has opened. One of the teachers I spoke to described her transformative experience: 'Within forty-five minutes of that first session, I was absolutely hooked.' This instant connection to coaching highlights its profound impact, not just in terms of professional development but also in fostering personal growth. Central to this empowerment is more than just acquiring new skills; it is about fostering teacher agency. Teacher agency is the capacity of educators to act purposefully and reflectively, making decisions that align with their values, expertise and the needs of their students. It is about educators feeling equipped, empowered to take ownership of their practice, adapt to challenges, and influence change within their classrooms and schools. It is about helping educators build the confidence, self-awareness and tools they need to navigate their roles effectively, not simply to meet the demands of teaching but to thrive – creating a richer and more fulfilling professional and personal life.

The connection between coaching and teacher agency has been the subject of increasing interest, especially through the work of scholars like Mark Priestley and Rachel Lofthouse. Their research emphasises the close link between ecological agency and coaching, particularly within the school context. Ecological agency is the understanding that teachers' actions are influenced not just by their internal motivations but also by the structures, relationships and the cultural context of their environment. Agency, therefore, isn't just about what an individual can do in isolation; it is about what they are empowered to do within the systems and communities they are part of. Coaching taps into this broader understanding of agency, helping teachers to reflect on their personal practices and navigate and influence the ecosystems in which they work.

Coaching and its role in education

Coaching plays a unique role in shaping the learning environment. Unlike traditional teaching, which focuses on content delivery, coaching creates a space where growth and development can truly flourish. When teachers feel empowered and have a strong sense of agency, they naturally adopt a coaching approach in their practice. The way coaching is introduced in a school can make all the difference. When teachers are given the opportunity to engage with coaching and understand its principles, the impact on their teaching practices, classroom management and overall sense of empowerment can be profound.

The power of ecological agency

Ecological agency recognises the unique qualities that teachers bring into the classroom – their experiences, beliefs and values. This model of agency highlights that a teacher's sense of agency is shaped not only by their environment but also by their own practices. It encourages educators to reflect on how their beliefs influence their teaching style and interactions with students.

Past research highlights a view on agency as something people possess. More recently, Biesta et al (2015) reference their ecological concept of agency as something that can be achieved. The ecological agency model helps us understand how teachers make purposeful decisions and take meaningful action in their work. It highlights three key elements that shape this ability: *past experiences, future goals, and current circumstances.*

1 **Past experiences (Iterational):** Teachers draw on their past experiences to guide their actions. The more varied and richer a teacher's experiences – such as working with different student needs, trying new teaching strategies, or collaborating with others – the more tools they have to handle challenges and make informed decisions.

2 **Future goals (Projective):** Agency also involves looking ahead. Teachers who can imagine different ways to improve their teaching, set meaningful goals, or create solutions for their students are more likely to feel empowered to act. For example, a teacher who envisions ways to engage a disengaged student is using this forward-thinking element of agency.

3 **Current circumstances (Practical-evaluative):** Agency happens in the here and now, where teachers must assess what's available to them – resources, support, or time – and decide the best way forward. For instance, a teacher might adapt a lesson on the spot based on how their students are responding or what resources they have.

This model shows that a teacher's ability to take meaningful action isn't just about their skills or knowledge – it's shaped by how their experiences, goals and current environment interact. Research by van der Heijden et al (2015) shows that teachers are often driven to make changes that benefit their classrooms or schools. To support this, schools can create environments where teachers feel encouraged to reflect on their past, think about future possibilities, and make decisions that work in their current context. When this happens, teachers are more likely to take ownership of their practice, feel confident, and create lasting positive change for their students.

For example, consider a teacher who may lack confidence in supporting a dyslexic student. Even with specialised training, if the teacher doesn't believe they can effectively teach that student their sense of agency remains limited. Coaching allows for an exploration of these underlying beliefs and helps teachers restructure their thinking. This process can lead to deeper understanding of their abilities, resulting in a more empowered approach to teaching.

Coaching as a tool for empowerment

Coaching is a powerful tool for driving significant change. It provides educators with the space to reflect on their beliefs, identify what might be holding them back, and develop strategies to overcome these challenges. When teachers engage in coaching, they often find that their sense of agency grows, which in turn positively impacts their students. And when teachers model a coaching approach, it is something that students pick up on – they start adopting similar behaviours in their interactions with others, creating a culture of growth and empowerment throughout the school.

Empowerment is a powerful concept in both coaching and education. When teachers and students feel empowered, they're more likely to take ownership of their learning and development. This sense of empowerment is essential for fostering a culture of growth and continuous improvement in schools. By integrating coaching into the school environment, we can create a space where both teachers and students are empowered to learn, grow and succeed.

What does empowerment through coaching look like?

Empowerment through coaching is made up of several key elements that work together to create a transformative experience.

Reconnection with professional goals

One of the first things coaching does is help teachers reconnect with their professional goals. In the hustle of day-to-day demands, it is easy to lose sight of the bigger picture. Coaching offers a space to step back, reflect and get clear on what truly matters. Teachers can re-examine their personal values, career aspirations and teaching philosophies – things that may have been buried under lesson plans. With this clarity, they often walk away re-energised, with a renewed sense of purpose driving their work. It is like realigning a compass that has been spinning in too many directions.

> ### Practical strategies
> - Introduce regular, dedicated coaching sessions focused on long-term goal setting and alignment with personal values.
> - Teachers could create vision boards or use reflective journals to track progress and recalibrate goals.
> - Schedule goal-mapping workshops or one-to-one coaching sessions that allow teachers to revisit and reflect on their teaching philosophies and personal aspirations.

Fostering ownership and confidence

Another essential piece of the empowerment puzzle is ownership. Coaching helps educators take control of their professional development. They set personal goals, and as they work towards them, they start to build a sense of self-efficacy – the belief that they can influence their outcomes. This new-found confidence doesn't stay confined to coaching sessions; it spills over into classrooms, relationships with colleagues and approaches to challenges. When teachers feel empowered, they are more proactive, more engaged and more willing to take risks that can lead to meaningful improvements.

> ### Practical strategies
> - Encourage teachers to set personal development plans that tie in with coaching. These plans should include specific, measurable goals that they can work towards; this fosters accountability and ownership.
> - Use a self-assessment tool to help teachers identify strengths and areas for improvement. Then, work with coaches to establish a step-by-step action plan that boosts confidence in their abilities.

Encouragement of self-reflection and goal setting

Effective coaching fosters a habit of ongoing self-reflection and goal setting, which is crucial for maintaining momentum. It is about continuously checking in with oneself, revisiting objectives, assessing progress and adjusting along the way. When teachers regularly engage in this reflective practice, they're not just reacting to challenges – they're actively shaping their responses and strategies. It is empowerment in action: taking control of one's own development, and addressing obstacles with a sense of purpose and determination.

> ### Practical strategies
> - Build 'reflection checkpoints' into the school year. These could be individual coaching reviews where teachers revisit goals and reflect on their development.
> - Teachers could maintain reflective journals as part of their professional growth portfolio.
> - Coaches could ask guided questions to prompt deeper reflection. For example, 'What has been my biggest challenge this term, and how did I overcome it?'

Personal growth and professional development

Then there is the growth factor. Coaching is not just about solving immediate problems or improving specific skills – it is about broader personal and professional development. Through the coaching process, teachers often discover new strengths, build new skills and gain fresh perspectives that enhance both their teaching and personal lives. This growth is crucial because it not only makes them more capable of meeting their own needs but those of their students too. In a sense, empowered teachers become more adaptable, more responsive and, ultimately, more effective in creating dynamic learning environments.

> **Practical strategies**
> - Align coaching with ongoing professional development initiatives. For example, offer workshops or peer-coaching sessions on emerging educational practices, ensuring that coaching stays relevant to the teacher's evolving needs.
> - Create coaching pairs or coaching circles where teachers can share insights, challenges and solutions, promoting collaborative professional growth.

Empowerment as a catalyst for educational change

Empowerment is a critical factor for educational change. When teachers feel empowered, they are more likely to embrace new practices, lead initiatives and become active participants in the evolution of their schools. Empowerment turns them into agents of change, driving positive transformations in their educational communities. And when that happens, everyone benefits – the teachers, the students and the broader school environment.

> **Practical strategies**
> - Encourage teachers to take leadership roles within the coaching programme, such as mentoring new coaches or leading school-wide coaching initiatives.
> - Develop a teacher-led innovation fund, where empowered teachers can apply for resources to implement school improvement projects inspired by their coaching outcomes.

Designing coaching programmes for empowerment

Given the importance of empowerment, coaching programmes should be designed with these key elements in mind. This means incorporating strategies that foster self-reflection, encourage continuous goal setting, and create opportunities for personal and professional growth. A well-designed coaching environment ensures teachers feel supported not only in improving their teaching practices but also in becoming more confident, self-aware and proactive in shaping their professional journeys. Coaching, at its core, is about transformation. It can take teachers on a journey of self-discovery where they can reconnect with their values, take ownership of their growth, and feel empowered to navigate their professional lives with clarity and confidence. This empowerment doesn't stop at the individual; it ripples outwards, contributing to school-wide improvements and creating a culture of continuous learning and development. In this way, coaching is not just a tool for teachers; it is a driving force for innovation, excellence and positive change in education.

> **Practical strategies**
> - Structure coaching programmes with built-in flexibility to adjust to the unique needs of teachers. Incorporate tools like strengths-based coaching or solution-focused techniques that allow teachers to address personal challenges in a way that empowers them.
> - Introduce strengths-based coaching assessments at the start of the coaching cycle to identify areas where teachers naturally excel and leverage those strengths in their teaching practice.

Summary
- This chapter explores the powerful connection between coaching and teacher agency.
- Ecological agency acknowledges the influence of teachers' beliefs, experiences and environments on their sense of agency.
- Coaching is a tool for educators to reflect on and reshape their beliefs, leading to increased empowerment, confidence and effectiveness.
- Teacher empowerment through coaching is fostered by reconnecting educators with their professional goals, encouraging ownership and self-efficacy and promoting ongoing self-reflection and goal setting.
- Coaching not only supports individual growth but also acts as a catalyst for positive change across the school community.
- Coaching programmes should be designed to support these elements to cultivate a culture of continuous learning and development in schools.

Reflection questions
1. How does my current belief system influence my sense of agency and effectiveness as an educator, and how might coaching help me explore and reshape these beliefs?
2. In what ways can I use coaching to reconnect with my professional goals?

3. How can I foster a habit of ongoing self-reflection and goal setting in my daily practice, and what impact might this have on my personal and professional growth?
4. What specific strategies can I employ to take greater ownership of my professional development, and how can coaching support me in this journey?
5. How can I contribute to creating a culture of empowerment and continuous learning in my school, and what role does coaching play in this process?

Chapter 4
Coaching competencies, frameworks and approaches: a personal exploration

Coaching is like a treasure trove filled with different models and frameworks, each offering its unique approach to helping coachees achieve their goals, gain self-awareness and foster personal growth. The beauty of coaching lies in understanding and applying these models in ways that can truly enhance the coaching experience. In this chapter, we are going to take a journey through some of the most prominent coaching frameworks and models, looking at where they come from, how they are used and why they matter – especially in educational settings.

ICF core competencies and their relevance

The International Coaching Federation (ICF) has established a set of core competencies (ICF, 2024) that set the gold standard for coaching practice. These competencies ensure that coaches adhere to high ethical standards and deliver meaningful outcomes for their coachees.

Some key ICF core competencies include:

- Establishing the coaching agreement: Creating a clear understanding of the coaching relationship, including roles, responsibilities and expectations.
- Establishing trust and intimacy: Building a strong, trusting relationship where coachees feel comfortable sharing openly.
- Coaching presence: Being fully present and responsive during coaching sessions, allowing the process to unfold naturally.
- Active listening: Understanding the underlying meaning, emotions and intentions behind what the coachee says.

- Powerful questioning: Asking thought-provoking questions that challenge assumptions and encourage deeper reflection.
- Direct communication: Delivering messages in a clear, impactful, and sensitive manner that considers the coachee's needs.
- Creating awareness: Helping coachees gain insights into their beliefs, behaviours and patterns.
- Designing actions: Collaborating with the coachee to create actionable steps that align with their goals and values.
- Planning and goal setting: Helping coachees develop a clear plan for achieving their goals.
- Managing progress and accountability: Tracking progress and holding the coachee accountable for their commitments.

These competencies are practical tools that guide coaches in delivering effective, impactful coaching. Whether working in education, corporate environments or personal development, adhering to these competencies ensures that we provide the highest standard of service to our coachees.

The EMCC and its competencies

The European Mentoring and Coaching Council (EMCC) is an organisation dedicated to promoting best practices in coaching and mentoring across Europe and beyond. It has developed a comprehensive set of competencies that serve as a benchmark for professional excellence in coaching and mentoring. These competencies are particularly valuable for ensuring that coaches adhere to high standards of practice and ethics.

Some key EMCC coaching and mentoring competencies include:

- Understanding self: This competency focuses on self-awareness, encouraging coaches to understand their own values, beliefs and biases. It is about recognising how these factors influence the coaching relationship and ensuring that personal perspectives don't unduly affect the coachee's journey.
- Commitment to self-development: Continuous personal and professional development is essential. Coaches are encouraged to engage in lifelong learning, reflecting on their practice, seeking feedback, and staying informed about new research and trends in coaching.
- Managing the contract: It is crucial to establish clear agreements about the coaching relationship, roles and expectations. This competency

ensures that both the coach and coachee have a shared understanding of the process and goals, which lays the foundation for effective coaching.
- Building the relationship: Developing a strong, trusting relationship is key to successful coaching. This involves creating a safe, supportive environment where the coachee feels valued and understood, allowing for open and honest communication.
- Enabling insight and learning: Coaches should facilitate the coachee's self-discovery and growth. This competency emphasises the importance of asking powerful questions, challenging assumptions and helping the coachee gain new perspectives and insights.
- Outcome and action orientation: Coaching should lead to tangible results. This competency focuses on helping the coachee translate insights into actionable steps, ensuring that the coaching process leads to meaningful change and progress.
- Use of models and techniques: A solid understanding of various coaching models and techniques is essential for effective practice. Coaches are encouraged to be flexible in their approach, adapting models to fit the coachee's unique needs and context.
- Evaluation: Regularly assessing the effectiveness of the coaching process is important for continuous improvement. This competency involves evaluating the outcomes of coaching sessions and making necessary adjustments to better support the coachee's goals.

The EMCC's competencies are a valuable resource for coaches at all levels, providing a clear framework for delivering high-quality coaching that is both ethical and impactful. By adhering to these competencies, coaches can ensure they are providing the best possible support to their coachees.

In summary, the ICF and EMCC competencies offer invaluable guidance for professional coaching, each providing a distinct yet complementary framework for effective practice. The ICF competencies focus on creating a structured, ethical and impactful coaching experience through skills like building trust, active listening and fostering accountability. Meanwhile, the EMCC competencies emphasise self-awareness, continuous learning, and the use of flexible approaches tailored to the coachee's unique needs. Together, these competencies highlight the importance of both personal and professional development in coaching, ensuring that coaches can build strong relationships, facilitate meaningful insights, and drive sustainable progress. By integrating these principles, coaches can elevate their practice and provide transformative support to their coachees.

The Global Framework for Coaching and Mentoring in Education

The Global Framework for Coaching and Mentoring in Education (van Nieuwerburgh et al., 2019) lays out a helpful model for how coaching can become an integral part of a school's culture. What I love about this framework is that it doesn't see coaching as something isolated or extra; it is about embedding coaching across all levels of the school community. In doing so, coaching becomes a natural, everyday practice that touches leadership, community, student experience and professional development. Let's take a closer look at how this works.

Educational leadership

Coaching is a powerful tool for school leaders, whether they are new to leadership or experienced veterans. One-to-one coaching helps leaders at every stage of their journey by providing them with the space to reflect on their leadership style and grow in their roles. Once leaders understand and practise coaching techniques, they naturally begin to use a coaching approach with their staff. It becomes part of their leadership identity. As van Nieuwerburgh (2014, p. 12) puts it, they adopt a coaching 'way of being'. At this point, coaching isn't just something leaders do; it becomes part of who they are.

Community engagement

Coaching is not just for the internal workings of a school. It can extend to how we engage with parents and the wider community. Teachers can use coaching approaches when working with parents, helping them develop their parenting skills. Parents can be trained in basic coaching techniques to use with their own children – coaching can bridge the gap between school and home in a meaningful way.

Student experience

At the heart of the Global Framework is student success and wellbeing. All these coaching interventions aim to support students in achieving their best, both academically and emotionally. Students can benefit from coaching directly, either by working with external coaches or school staff who have been trained to coach. Students can even be trained to coach each other, creating a peer-to-peer support system. When students coach one another, both coach and coachee gain something valuable. For example, research has shown that student coaches develop a more positive attitude towards learning (van Nieuwerburgh and Tong, 2013, p. 20).

Professional practice

When it comes to professional practice, coaching is a game changer. At its core, coaching helps teachers grow by improving their teaching and learning strategies. Whether the coaching comes from external experts, senior leaders or peers, it's about creating a culture where teachers see coaching as a catalyst for their own learning and development. Peer coaching among teachers can focus on anything from classroom techniques to pastoral care, depending on what is most relevant to their current challenges.

Some schools even designate instructional coaches (Knight, 2007), whose role is to guide teachers through specific instructional practices using a dialogic approach (Knight, 2018). This approach emphasises open, two-way conversations where both the coach and the teacher actively contribute to the learning process. Unlike a more facilitative coaching style, where the coach primarily asks questions to help the coachee reflect and find their own answers, the dialogic approach is more collaborative. It involves the coach sharing expertise, offering suggestions and engaging in a balanced dialogue to co-construct new ideas or strategies with the teacher.

In a dialogic coaching session, both parties explore the topic together, combining the coach's knowledge and the teacher's insights about their own classroom. This differs from the facilitative approach, which encourages more self-directed discovery by the coachee, and relies heavily on asking powerful, open-ended questions without steering the conversation. While the facilitative approach fosters greater autonomy and self-reflection in the teacher, the dialogic method supports more direct skill-building and practical guidance, especially when the goal is to implement specific instructional techniques to improve teaching and learning outcomes.

The distinction between these two methods is key: the facilitative coaching that my book focuses on is designed to empower individuals to uncover their own solutions through deep reflection and questioning, whereas the dialogic approach involves more guidance, shared knowledge and co-created solutions. Both approaches have their place in education, depending on the goals and the level of support the teacher needs.

The Global Framework for Coaching and Mentoring in Education has a holistic approach. Coaching is integrated into all aspects of school life, from leadership and community to student experience and professional practice. The coaching interventions that we put in place influence the school environment and, in turn, the environment shapes how coaching evolves. It is a dynamic, ongoing process that brings the whole school community together in a shared journey of growth and development.

The GROW model

The GROW model (Whitmore, 2009) has become a cornerstone in the coaching world due to its simplicity, versatility and effectiveness. Widely regarded as one of the most accessible and impactful coaching frameworks, it provides a clear structure for guiding conversations and fostering meaningful progress. GROW (Goal, Reality, Options, and Will) offers a step-by-step approach that helps coachees clarify their objectives, explore their current situation, identify potential strategies, and commit to actionable steps.

Its straightforward structure makes it particularly valuable for coaches working in a variety of contexts, from education and personal development to leadership and team coaching. The GROW model encourages deep reflection and problem-solving, empowering coachees to take ownership of their growth while keeping the process focused and forward-moving. By balancing support and challenge, it enables coaches to create a safe yet dynamic environment where coachees can unlock their potential and achieve meaningful outcomes.

Goal

First, you need to identify what your coachee wants to achieve by setting SMART goals: Specific, Measurable, Achievable, Relevant and Time-bound (see chapter 6 for further details). As a coach, your job is to help the coachee articulate their true objectives, aligning these goals with their values and long-term vision.

- **What specifically would you like to achieve by the end of this coaching session?**

    This question encourages the coachee to focus on a clear and immediate outcome, helping them define a specific and actionable goal for the session. It sets a purposeful tone and ensures both the coach and coachee are aligned on what success looks like in the short term.

- **How does this goal connect to your broader vision or long-term aspirations?**

    This question prompts the coachee to reflect on the bigger picture and align their goal with their values and long-term objectives. It helps them ensure that their immediate goal is meaningful and relevant, which can increase motivation and commitment to achieving it.

Reality

In the Reality stage of the GROW model, the coach's role is to help the coachee gain a clear, objective understanding of their current situation. This involves asking thoughtful questions that encourage the coachee to reflect on their strengths, challenges and any obstacles they may face.

Here are some example questions a coach might ask during this stage:

- **How would you describe the current situation?**

    This question helps the coachee ground their thinking in the present moment and begin to explore their current reality.

- **Can you walk me through how you have approached this goal so far?**

    This question encourages the coachee to reflect on their progress and take stock of what has or hasn't worked.

- **In which areas do you feel most confident right now?**

    This focuses on the coachee's assets, helping them recognise the resources they already have at their disposal.

- **Are there any obstacles that you feel are particularly challenging at the moment?**

    This helps the coachee identify any roadblocks or difficulties they need to overcome.

- **Who can support you in achieving your goal, and how might they help?**

    Encourages the coachee to think about their support network.

- **Where do you think you are getting stuck or held back?**

    Helps the coachee explore areas where they may feel blocked or frustrated.

- **How are you currently managing these obstacles?**

    Prompts reflection on how the coachee is handling challenges and whether adjustments are needed.

- **If you continue on your current path, where do you see yourself in a month?**

    Encourages forward thinking based on their current reality, potentially highlighting the need for change.

- **Can you share an example of when you have faced a similar situation, and how you handled it?**

    Draws out past experiences and patterns that might inform their current situation.

- **How does this situation align with your long-term values or priorities?**

    Helps the coachee assess whether their current reality aligns with their broader life goals or values.

Options

In this phase, you and the coachee explore possible actions and strategies to bridge the gap between reality and the goal. Encourage them to think creatively and widely at this point. The goal is to generate as many options as possible before narrowing down to the most viable and appealing ones.

Here are some example questions a coach might ask during this stage:

- **How could you approach this challenge in a completely different way?**

    This invites the coachee to break away from their usual thinking and consider fresh, unconventional solutions they might not otherwise have thought of.

- **If you had unlimited resources, how might you solve this?**

    Encourages the coachee to think big, without the usual constraints of time, money or expertise, opening up creative possibilities.

- **Who could offer support or guidance as you explore these options?**

    Prompts the coachee to consider who in their network – colleagues, mentors, friends – could provide valuable insights, resources or encouragement.

- **What would be the first step you could take towards your goal?**

    Helps the coachee identify an immediate, actionable step they could take to start moving towards their goal, building momentum.

- **Can you think of an approach you've seen someone else use successfully?**

    Encourages the coachee to reflect on strategies or tactics they have observed in others, which could provide inspiration for their own situation.

- **How do you feel about the different options you have considered so far?**

    This question taps into the coachee's emotions, helping them gauge which options resonate most with them on an emotional level, which is often a good indicator of motivation.

- **Which option would feel most energising or motivating for you?**

    A follow-up that narrows the focus to the option that generates the most enthusiasm, as this is likely to be the one they feel most committed to pursuing.

- **Are there any risks or downsides you see with these choices?**

    Encourages the coachee to think critically about the potential challenges or drawbacks of each option, helping them weigh the pros and cons effectively.

- **If you had to make progress by tomorrow, what action would you choose to take?**

    Adds a sense of urgency, which can help the coachee focus on practical, immediate options instead of overthinking possibilities.

- **Where could you find additional resources or information to support these options?**

    Prompts the coachee to consider what further information or resources they might need to make an informed decision, encouraging a proactive approach to gathering support.

Will (or Way Forward)

Finally, the focus is on commitment. This is where you help the coachee choose the best options and develop a concrete action plan, complete with timelines and accountability measures. This stage ensures that the coachee leaves the session with a clear sense of direction and the motivation to take the next steps.

Here are some example questions a coach might ask during this stage:

- **Which of the options we have discussed feels most achievable and motivating for you?**

    Encourages the coachee to choose the option they feel most ready to act on.

- **What specific steps will you take to move forward with this plan?**

    Helps the coachee break down their goal into clear, actionable steps.

- **When will you begin taking these steps, and what is your timeline for completing them?**

    Establishes a concrete time frame for action.

- **How will you hold yourself accountable for following through on these actions?**

    Encourages the coachee to take responsibility for their progress.

- **What resources or support do you need to ensure you can complete these steps?**

    Prompts the coachee to think about what additional help or tools they may need.

- **On a scale of 1–10, how committed are you to taking these actions?**

    Helps assess the coachee's level of commitment and motivation.

- **What might get in the way of you achieving these steps, and how will you overcome those obstacles?**

    Encourages the coachee to anticipate and plan for potential challenges.

- **How will you measure your progress along the way?**

    Prompts the coachee to think about how they will track their success.

- **Who could help keep you accountable or offer support during this process?**

    Encourages the coachee to consider involving others for accountability or encouragement.

- **What will be your first step, and when will you take it?**

    This gets the coachee to commit to an immediate next step, reinforcing their momentum and motivation.

The GROW model is structured yet flexible by nature, making it a go-to approach in various coaching contexts, whether in business, personal development or education.

The GROWTH model

The GROWTH model (Goal, Reality, Options, Will, Tactics and Habits), developed by Growth Coaching International (van Nieuwerburgh, 2020), takes everything good about GROW and adds some extra layers, making it perfect for situations where ongoing development and long-term change are the goals – think educational leadership or professional growth.

Goal

Just like in GROW, we start with setting a clear and motivating goal. But in this case, there's a stronger focus on aligning this goal with the coachee's broader life or career aspirations, ensuring that it contributes to their overall wellbeing and fulfilment.

- **What is the most meaningful outcome you hope to achieve, and how will this contribute to your broader aspirations?**

  This question encourages the coachee to think beyond immediate tasks or challenges and connect their goal to a larger sense of purpose. It fosters reflection on what truly matters to them and ensures the goal is aligned with their long-term aspirations and values.

- **If you achieve this goal, how will it impact your sense of well-being or fulfilment?**

  This question helps the coachee evaluate the emotional and personal significance of their goal. By considering the broader impact on their life, they can assess whether the goal is worth pursuing and make adjustments if necessary to ensure it aligns with their overall wellbeing.

Reality

The exploration of the current situation in the GROWTH model goes deeper. Coaches are encouraged to look beyond immediate obstacles and consider bigger factors that might affect the coachee's progress, like organisational culture or external influences.

- **What challenges or barriers do you see right now, and how might external circumstances be influencing these?**

  This question encourages deeper reflection on external influences, such as workplace dynamics, policies or societal pressures, enabling them to better understand the context of their challenges.

- **What resources, relationships or support systems could you draw on to navigate these challenges?**

  This question shifts the coachee's focus from limitations to opportunities and strengths. It enables them to identify existing tools or networks that can help them overcome barriers, fostering a sense of agency and possibility in their current situation.

Options

During this phase, the coachee explores short-term and long-term strategies, looking at what they can do right now, and at resources, personal strengths and external support systems that can help them along the way.

- **What are some immediate actions you could take to start moving toward your goal?**

    This question helps the coachee focus on practical, short-term strategies they can implement right away. It encourages them to break their goal into manageable steps, reducing overwhelm and building momentum.

- **What resources, strengths or support systems can you draw on to help you achieve both your short-term and long-term goals?**

    This question encourages the coachee to reflect on the assets they already have, such as personal skills, relationships, or external tools. It shifts the focus from barriers to possibilities and empowers them to see how they can leverage what is already available to them.

Will

Commitment to action is still the focus here, but the GROWTH model also emphasises resilience and adaptability. This is about helping the coachee anticipate challenges and plan for them, ensuring they stay motivated even when things don't go as planned.

- **What specific steps will you commit to taking and when will you take them?**

    This question helps the coachee clarify their plan of action and make a firm commitment to specific, time-bound tasks. It translates their ideas into tangible steps, reinforcing accountability and ensuring momentum.

- **What challenges or obstacles might come up and how can you prepare to handle them?**

    This question encourages the coachee to think ahead and anticipate potential setbacks. It promotes resilience by helping them develop strategies to stay on track, even if things don't go as planned.

Tactics

Here is where GROWTH really diverges from GROW. Tactics involve detailed planning of how to implement the chosen actions. This could include setting specific milestones, identifying necessary resources, and establishing routines or habits that support the goal.

Here are some example questions a coach might ask during this stage:

- **What specific milestones will help you track progress towards your goal?**

    Encourages the coachee to define measurable points that indicate success along the way.

- **What routines or habits do you need to establish to support your actions?**

    Helps the coachee identify daily or weekly habits that will make achieving the goal more manageable.

- **What resources, tools or support do you need to put these actions into motion?**

    Prompts the coachee to think about what tangible resources they will need to succeed.

- **How can you break this goal down into smaller, actionable tasks?**

    Guides the coachee to deconstruct their goal into bite-sized, manageable actions.

- **Who can support you in achieving these tactics, and how can you involve them?**

    Encourages the coachee to consider who could help them along the way.

- **What systems or structures can you put in place to ensure you stay on track?**

    Prompts the coachee to think about creating accountability systems or organising frameworks.

- **How will you prioritise these actions among your other commitments?**

    Encourages the coachee to think about how they will integrate the goal into their existing responsibilities.

- **What will be the first action you take, and when will you start?**

    Helps the coachee clarify the very first step they need to take to begin moving forward.

- **How will you know if a tactic isn't working, and what will you do if you need to adjust?**

    Prepares the coachee for flexibility and adaptation if plans don't go as expected.

- **What time frame will you set for completing each milestone, and how will you celebrate achieving them?**

  Prompts the coachee to set timelines and also consider celebrating progress, which reinforces motivation.

Habits

Finally, we focus on creating sustainable habits that reinforce the desired changes. The coach works with the coachee to integrate new behaviours into their daily life, making sure that the progress made during coaching is maintained over the long term.

Here are some example questions a coach might ask during this stage:

- **What daily or weekly habits will help you maintain the progress you've made?**

  Encourages the coachee to identify specific, recurring actions that will reinforce their goals.

- **How can you incorporate these new behaviours into your existing routines?**

  Helps the coachee think about how to seamlessly fit new habits into their current lifestyle.

- **What small actions can you take each day to ensure continued momentum?**

  Focuses on identifying easy, consistent steps the coachee can take to build their new habits.

- **What triggers or cues can you use to remind yourself to practise these habits?**

  Encourages the coachee to establish reminders that will prompt them to perform their new habits.

- **In what ways will you stay accountable for maintaining these habits in the long term?**

  Prompts the coachee to think about mechanisms to track their adherence to the new habits.

- **What challenges do you anticipate in sticking to these habits, and how will you overcome them?**

  Helps the coachee prepare for obstacles and develop strategies to stay consistent.

- **Who could support or check in with you to help reinforce these habits?**

  Encourages the coachee to seek external support for maintaining their new behaviours.

- **How will you recognise when these habits have become part of your regular routine?**

  Helps the coachee define what success looks like in terms of habitual behaviour.

- **If you miss a day of practising your new habits, how will you get back on track?**

  Encourages a plan for resilience and bouncing back after setbacks.

- **How will you reward yourself or celebrate when you consistently stick to your habits?**

  Prompts the coachee to build in incentives that keep them motivated as they work to solidify new behaviours.

The GROWTH model's emphasis on tactics and habits makes it particularly valuable when long-term behaviour change and continuous improvement are key objectives, especially in leadership coaching or personal development.

Clean Language and Clean Setup

Clean Language

Clean Language is a unique and transformative approach developed by David Grove in the 1980s. What makes Clean Language stand out is its focus on minimising the coach's influence, allowing the coachee's own words, metaphors and experiences to guide the entire process. This method creates a space where the coachee can uncover and explore their own thoughts, emotions and deeper beliefs.

The real power of Clean Language lies in its ability to help coachees unearth deep-seated beliefs and emotional patterns that might remain hidden in more directive coaching approaches. By using their own words and metaphors, coachees can access new levels of insight, often revealing things they were not consciously aware of before. It encourages self-discovery without interference from the coach, making it an especially useful tool for exploring complex issues that might be difficult to articulate.

Clean Language is built on open-ended, non-directive questions that allow coachees to stay in control of their narrative. Some of the key questions include:

- 'What would you like to have happen?'
- 'What will _____ be like?'
- 'What will you need to be like for _____ to be like that?'
- 'What support and resources will you need?'

These questions gently nudge the coachee to explore their thoughts and emotions, but without the coach imposing any interpretations. It's a subtle yet powerful approach that encourages clarity and authenticity, helping coachees find their own solutions and insights. The beauty of Clean Language lies in its neutrality – it allows the coachee's language and experience to lead the way, creating a truly non-judgemental and open space.

Clean Setup: extending the principles

Clean Setup takes the principles of Clean Language and extends them to the overall coaching process. It is about ensuring that the entire coaching environment – both the physical space and the relational dynamics – are focused on the coachee's agenda. Clean Setup involves setting up the conditions that allow the coachee to feel safe, supported and in control of their own journey. This might include things like discussing the coaching contract, agreeing on confidentiality, and clarifying the roles and expectations of both coach and coachee.

For example, at the start of a coaching relationship, using Clean Setup might look like:

- agreeing on the purpose and goals of the coaching sessions
- setting clear boundaries around confidentiality, and what will or won't be shared with others
- clarifying the roles of both coach and coachee – ensuring that the coachee understands that they are the expert in their own life and that the coach is there to facilitate, not direct.

By creating this clear and transparent foundation, Clean Setup helps ensure that the coachee remains at the centre of the process, with a strong sense of ownership over their own learning and development.

Clean Language and Clean Setup in educational settings

In the world of education, both Clean Language and Clean Setup offer powerful tools for teachers, school leaders and even students. Often, educators and leaders have underlying beliefs and assumptions about teaching, learning and leadership that influence their behaviours and decision-making – beliefs they may not even be consciously aware of. Clean Language helps them gently uncover and explore these underlying beliefs, leading to deeper insights and more sustainable solutions. For example, a school leader might discover through Clean Language coaching that their resistance to a new initiative stems from a deep-seated belief about their role or responsibility in the school community. A teacher might uncover an emotional barrier that has been holding them back from trying new approaches in the classroom. By using Clean Language, they are empowered to explore these beliefs on their own terms, leading to more authentic and lasting change.

Clean Setup can also be incredibly effective in educational environments. By ensuring that the coaching process is clearly defined and aligned with the educator's own goals, Clean Setup helps create a trusting and collaborative relationship between coach and coachee. This is especially important in schools, where there may be additional layers of hierarchy or expectations that need to be navigated. Clean Setup ensures that the coaching is fully focused on the individual's needs, helping educators feel more empowered and engaged in their own growth.

At their core, Clean Language and Clean Setup offer a gentle but powerful way of facilitating self-discovery, clarity and sustainable change. By minimising the coach's influence and allowing the coachee to lead the way, these approaches create a safe and open space for deep reflection and growth. Whether used in educational settings or in other coaching contexts, Clean Language and Clean Setup help individuals tap into their own wisdom, uncover underlying beliefs and, ultimately, find the solutions that work best for them. In a world where so many coaching models emphasise direction and structure, Clean Language reminds us of the power of listening deeply and trusting the coachee's own process. It is a beautiful reminder that sometimes the most profound insights come not from being told what to do, but from being given the space to discover it for ourselves.

Clean Setup in action

Coach:

'Before we begin, let's take a few moments to ensure we are all aligned and clear about the purpose of this session. This process is about exploring your ideas and finding solutions that work best for you, without any external judgements or imposed ideas.'

- **'What would you like to have happen in today's session?'**

    Allows the coachee to state their individual or collective goals, helping the coach understand their intentions for the session.

- **'How will you know when this session has been useful to you?'**

    Encourages the coachee to think about what success looks like by the end of the session, clarifying their expectations.

- **'What needs to be in place for you to feel comfortable and open in this conversation?'**

    Ensures a safe and trusting environment by asking the coachee to reflect on what conditions will support them best.

- **'What is the best way for me, as your coach, to support you during this session?'**

    Puts the responsibility in the hands of the coachee for how they'd like the coach to interact – whether they prefer more guiding questions, active listening or gentle challenges.

- **'What might you need to let go of or put aside to fully engage in this session?'**

    Helps the coachee become aware of any distractions, stress or preconceived notions that may prevent them from participating fully.

- **'What's the most useful outcome you can imagine from this session?'**

    Encourages the coachee to envision an ideal result, helping them focus on their broader aspirations.

- **'How will we know when you've made progress?'**

    Reinforces the need for observable progress markers during the session and encourages the coachee to define what that looks like.

- **'What would you like to happen after this session to continue moving forward?'**

  Encourages the coachee to think about follow-up actions or sustained habits that will help them carry their learning forward.

Integrating coaching models into practice

Applying coaching models in real-world scenarios requires flexibility, creativity and an understanding of the coachee's unique context. As coaches, we need to be adept at selecting and adapting models to suit the specific needs of our coachees and the situations they face.

- Contextual sensitivity: Being attuned to the specific challenges and opportunities within the coachee's environment is crucial. For example, in a school setting, we might need to consider the broader educational landscape, including policies, school culture and community dynamics.
- Combining models: Sometimes, a single coaching model is not enough to address the complexities of a coachee's situation. It can be beneficial to combine elements from different models, like integrating the GROW model with Clean Language techniques, to provide both structure and the flexibility needed to explore deeper issues.
- Continuous learning: Coaching is an ever-evolving field, with new models, techniques and research emerging regularly. Staying open to learning, and integrating new approaches into our practice, ensures that we continue to provide the best possible support to our coachees.

Coaching models are invaluable tools that guide the coaching process, providing structure, clarity and direction. Whether using the GROW model for straightforward goal setting, the GROWTH model for deeper, long-term development, or Clean Language for exploring complex inner landscapes, these frameworks empower coachees to achieve their goals and unlock their potential.

In educational settings, coaching can transform not only individual educators but also entire school communities. By integrating coaching models into school culture, educators can foster a more supportive, collaborative and growth-oriented environment that benefits both staff and students. As coaches, our role is to remain adaptable, continuously refining our approach to meet the evolving needs of our coachees and the contexts in which we work. By mastering a range of coaching models and competencies, we can deliver impactful coaching that leads to lasting change and positive outcomes for all involved.

Summary

- Coaching models and frameworks can help coachees achieve goals, gain self-awareness and foster personal growth.
- Foundational frameworks, like the ICF core competencies and EMCC's competencies, guide coaches in ethical practice and effective coaching.
- The GROW and GROWTH models are highlighted for their structured, goal-oriented approaches, with GROWTH adding a focus on long-term development.
- Clean Language is a model that minimises coach influence, encouraging coachees to explore their beliefs and emotions using their own language.
- Flexibility in applying coaching models is essential, with a focus on adapting to different coaching contexts, particularly in educational settings.
- Coaches are encouraged to blend models, tailor their approach to coachees' needs, and engage in continuous learning to refine their practices for meaningful, lasting change.

Reflection questions

1. How do you decide which coaching model or framework to apply in different coaching situations, and how does that choice impact your coachee's experience?
2. How can you blend elements from different coaching models to better support the unique needs of your coachees?
3. In what ways do the ICF and EMCC competencies guide your coaching practice, and how might you strengthen your alignment with these standards?
4. How comfortable are you with using non-directive approaches like Clean Language in your coaching, and how might this technique enhance your coachees' self-discovery?
5. How do you ensure that your coaching remains adaptable and responsive to the evolving needs of your coachees, particularly in educational settings?

Chapter 5
Coaching contracting: setting the stage for success

Starting your coaching journey, whether personally or within a school setting, is an exciting step towards growth and development. Over the past decade, numerous online and face-to-face courses have emerged, offering coaching training across various fields: leadership coaching, life coaching, business coaching and more. These programmes are designed to equip individuals with the skills needed to create a space for focused, solutions-oriented conversations. Whether you are seeking to develop these skills yourself or looking for a qualified coach to guide you, it is crucial to understand the importance of the initial steps in the coaching process.

One of the first and most important steps in any coaching relationship is the initial conversation, often referred to as a 'coaching contracting' conversation. This is where you and your potential coach get to know each other and determine if you are a good fit. This meeting is essential because it sets the tone for the entire coaching journey. It is a chance to explore the coach's approach, understand how they operate and decide whether their style aligns with what you are looking for. During this conversation, the coach will probably ask you about your goals: what you want to achieve, what is currently working well and what areas you would like to see improvement in. This discussion helps to clarify your needs and gives you a taste of how coaching might help you move forward with something you have been thinking about for a while. It is an opportunity to experience first-hand how coaching can help mobilise your thinking and inspire progress.

The importance of establishing a coaching contract

Once you have decided to move forward with a coach, it is essential to establish a clear contract. This agreement lays the foundation for your coaching relationship, ensuring that all necessary details are agreed upon so that the focus can remain on your development. Effective contracting clarifies mutual expectations, and outlines how you and your coach will work together.

Key aspects of the coaching contract include:

- Ground rules: Establishing basic guidelines for the coaching relationship.
- Duration, timing and frequency: Deciding how long sessions will last, when they will occur and how often you will meet.
- Coaching programme or individual sessions: Determining whether you will follow a structured programme or take a more flexible, session-by-session approach.
- Fees: If your coaching sessions are being outsourced by an external coach you will need to clarify the cost of the coaching sessions.
- Code of ethics: Ensuring that both parties understand and agree to adhere to ethical guidelines.
- Contact between sessions: Setting expectations for communication outside of scheduled sessions.
- Cancellations: Agreeing on policies for rescheduling or cancelling sessions.

The chemistry session: finding the right fit

The relationship between a coach and a coachee is deeply personal, and its success depends heavily on the chemistry between the two. The 'chemistry session' is your opportunity to determine if you and the coach are a good match. Here is how this first meeting typically unfolds:

1. Building rapport: From the first interaction, whether it's a phone call, an email or a meeting, the goal is to establish trust and make the client feel heard and valued.
2. Clarifying the session's purpose: Explain that this session is an opportunity to see if you're a good fit for each other and to outline what coaching involves.
3. Sharing backgrounds: The coach will share their qualifications, experience and coaching philosophy to give you a sense of who they are and how they work.
4. Discussing practicalities: This includes talking about session frequency, fee structure, and any reports or follow-up communications.
5. Exploring the coachee goals: The coach will ask about your primary goals and what you hope to achieve through coaching.

6. Defining success: The coach will ask what needs to happen during this session for you to feel confident about moving forward together.
7. Listening without judgement: The coach will focus on understanding your perspective without immediately providing answers or solutions.
8. Avoiding unrealistic promises: The coach will be clear about what coaching can and cannot achieve, to manage expectations.
9. Deciding on next steps: If both parties agree to move forward, the next session will be scheduled and any preparatory work outlined.
10. Reflecting on the experience: After the session, both you and the coach should reflect on the interaction to ensure it is the right fit.

By the end of the chemistry session, you should feel more informed about what coaching entails and whether this coach is the right guide for your journey. A successful session leaves both coach and coachee excited and ready to embark on the coaching process together.

Boundaries and expectations

Another critical part of the contract involves setting boundaries. It is important to distinguish between coaching, therapy, training and supervision, as each has a different focus and purpose. Establishing these boundaries helps manage expectations and ensures the coachee understands what coaching offers and what it does not.

- **Coaching:** Coaching is a collaborative process focused on helping individuals achieve specific goals, enhance performance, and foster personal or professional growth. It is future-oriented, with an emphasis on setting objectives, exploring options, and taking action. Coaches act as facilitators, guiding coachees to uncover their own solutions rather than providing direct answers.
- **Therapy:** Therapy is primarily focused on healing and addressing emotional, psychological, or behavioural issues that may stem from past experiences. It often delves into understanding and resolving the root causes of problems, with a goal of achieving emotional wellbeing and healing. Therapists are trained mental health professionals who work within a clinical framework.
- **Training:** Training is about imparting knowledge or teaching specific skills. It is typically a structured process with a clear curriculum, where the trainer acts as the expert, providing guidance and instruction. The focus is on transferring expertise to the learner, often in a group setting.

- **Supervision:** Supervision is a process of providing professional support and oversight to individuals, such as coaches, therapists, or educators, to ensure they maintain high standards of practice. It focuses on reflecting on their work, improving their skills, and addressing challenges in their professional roles. Supervisors often act as mentors, offering constructive feedback and guidance.

Clearly defining these distinctions during the contracting phase helps coachees understand that coaching is not a substitute for therapy, a training programme, or professional supervision. By setting these boundaries, coaches create a transparent and ethical foundation for the coaching relationship, ensuring both parties are aligned and the process remains focused on the coachee's specific goals and needs.

The contract should also cover confidentiality agreements, any involvement of a line manager or third party in the coaching process, and clearly defined roles for both the coach and the coachee.

The logistics of where and how the coaching sessions will take place – whether face to face, via phone or through video calls – are also important to clarify. Additionally, you and your coach should discuss and agree on the goals of the coaching, the methodologies that will be used and any preparation required before sessions.

Work between sessions

Coaching does not end when the session is over. The time between sessions is an essential part of the coaching journey, providing opportunities to integrate insights and put plans into action. You might engage in activities that reinforce your learning and progress, such as journaling to reflect on your thoughts and emotions, practising new skills to build confidence, or completing specific exercises designed to help you move closer to your goals.

This 'homework' is about fostering accountability and ownership of your growth. For example, you might experiment with a new communication style at work, track your progress toward a fitness goal, or practice mindfulness techniques to reduce stress. These activities allow you to test ideas in real-world settings, bringing valuable experiences back to your next coaching session for deeper exploration.

Regular self-assessment and maintaining open communication with your coach can further enhance your growth. Sharing insights, challenges, and successes between sessions helps to refine your strategies and ensures the coaching remains aligned with your evolving needs. By staying engaged and proactive, you maximise the impact of the coaching process, turning moments of reflection and action into sustained personal and professional development.

Summary

- The initial contracting conversation is a critical step in the coaching process, laying the foundation for a successful coaching relationship.
- Establishing a clear and well-defined contract ensures that both coach and coachee are aligned on goals, expectations and the coaching process.
- The chemistry session is crucial for determining whether coach and coachee are a good fit to work together.
- Open communication and setting clear expectations during contracting are essential for building trust and ensuring mutual understanding.
- A well-structured contract enables both coach and coachee to start the coaching journey with confidence and clarity.

Reflection questions

1. What are the most important qualities you are looking for in a coach, and how can you assess these during the initial conversation?
2. How do you feel about the goals you have set for coaching, and how might these evolve as you work with your coach?
3. What concerns or hesitations do you have about starting a coaching journey, and how can you address these in the chemistry session?
4. In what ways do you think a clear and detailed coaching contract can enhance your coaching experience?
5. How do you plan to stay engaged and proactive between coaching sessions to maximise your growth and development?

Chapter 6
Charting the path: visioning and goal setting in coaching

As coaches, one of the most impactful ways we can support our coachees is by helping them clarify their vision and set meaningful goals. This process is about uncovering what truly drives the coachee, what they aspire to, and how they can move forward with purpose and intention. A coaching session without clear goals can feel like wandering without direction, but with the right goal in place, everything becomes more focused and achievable. I have always found that the moment a coachee sets a clear goal, it is like a light bulb goes on. They move from talking about what has been bothering them to then actively working towards something. This chapter focuses on how we, as coaches, can guide coachees through that crucial step of visioning and goal setting, ensuring they leave each session with clarity and a sense of purpose.

The importance of visioning and goal setting

An important step in any successful coaching journey is understanding where the coachee wants to go. But this is not always as straightforward as it sounds. Sometimes, coachees arrive at a session with a general sense of dissatisfaction or a vague desire for change, but they are not yet sure what they want to achieve. Other times, they have a goal in mind but have not fully clarified it or don't yet see how they can achieve it.

This is where visioning comes in. Visioning allows the coachee to tap into their deeper aspirations and start to imagine what success looks like for them. From there, we can guide them to set clear, actionable goals that give them a roadmap to follow. A strong goal includes what the coachee wants to achieve and the steps they will take to get there.

Practical strategies

Create space for reflection

Begin by asking the coachee to take a moment to reflect on what is most pressing for them at that moment. Invite them to think about:

- What's on your mind today?
- What do you feel is the most important thing for us to focus on in this session?

This step helps the coachee surface their immediate thoughts and concerns, allowing them to narrow down what is truly important.

The visioning prompt

After the initial reflection, guide the coachee through a visioning exercise:

- Imagine it is the end of this session, and everything has gone exactly as you had hoped. You've achieved what you set out to accomplish. What does that look like? How do you feel? Encourage the coachee to describe their ideal outcome in detail, prompting them with questions like:
- What specific change has taken place?
- How are you thinking, feeling or behaving differently?
- What does this success mean for you going forward?

This process helps coachees clarify what they really want out of the session and connects them to the deeper motivations behind their goals.

From vision to goal

Now that the coachee has a clear vision of their desired outcome, help them refine it into a concrete goal for the session:

- Based on what you've shared, what specific goal can we focus on today to bring you closer to that vision? Encourage the coachee to articulate a goal that is both actionable and meaningful. For example, instead of 'I want to feel less overwhelmed', they might set a goal like 'I want to identify three strategies to manage my workload more effectively.'

Ask clarifying questions to sharpen the goal:

- What exactly would you like to achieve today?
- What steps will help you move towards this goal?
- What will success look like for you by the end of the session?

> Once the coachee has articulated their goal, confirm it by repeating it back to them:
> - So, your goal for today is to [state the goal]. Does that feel clear and achievable? After confirmation, encourage them to commit to working towards that goal during the session.

This visioning process is about creating an emotional connection to that goal. When coachees can visualise success, they become more invested in the steps they will need to take to achieve it.

The SMART goal-setting approach

Once the coachee has a clear vision of their goal, it is time to make sure that goal is actionable and realistic. The SMART goal-setting approach is a widely used framework that helps coachees ensure their goals are Specific, Measurable, Achievable, Relevant and Time-bound.

> ### Practical strategies
> Here is how you can guide your coachee through the SMART framework:
>
> **Specific**
> - Help the coachee narrow down their goal to something specific. A vague goal like 'I want to be more organised' might be reframed as 'I want to create a daily to-do list to prioritise tasks.'
> - Ask clarifying questions:
>   - What exactly do you want to achieve?
>   - Who is involved? What are the key actions?
>
> **Measurable**
> - Ask the coachee to define how they will measure progress. For example, 'I will know I am more organised when I can stick to my to-do list for a week.'
> - Measuring success helps the coachee stay motivated and track their progress over time.

Achievable
- Ensure the goal is realistic. Help the coachee assess whether they have the resources, time and capability to achieve the goal.
- Ask, 'Is this something you feel confident you can achieve within the time frame?'

Relevant
- Make sure the goal aligns with the coachee's broader objectives or values. A goal that does not connect with their larger aspirations might lack motivation.
- Ask, 'How does this goal fit into the bigger picture of what you want to achieve?'

Time-bound
- Help the coachee set a clear deadline for their goal. This could be by the end of the session or a longer-term deadline, depending on the nature of the goal.
- Ask, 'When do you want to achieve this?'

The SMART framework is a practical tool that makes goal setting more structured, ensuring that the coachee has a clear pathway towards achieving their objectives.

Summary

- Coaching helps coachees clarify their vision and set meaningful, actionable goals during sessions.
- The visioning process is introduced as a tool to guide coachees in connecting with their deeper aspirations and envisioning success.
- The SMART goal-setting approach is presented as a structured framework, ensuring goals are Specific, Measurable, Achievable, Relevant and Time-bound.
- Creating a clear sense of direction for coachees is emphasised, helping them move from vague desires to well-defined goals.
- Practical exercises and strategies are provided to help coaches foster a sense of purpose and support coachees in taking ownership of their growth.
- Coaching ensures that coachees receive the guidance and support necessary to achieve lasting outcomes from their efforts.

Reflection questions
1. How do you currently guide coachees in clarifying their vision for success, and what strategies could enhance that process?
2. When helping a coachee set goals, how do you ensure that their goals are both meaningful and actionable?
3. What challenges have you faced when working with coachees who struggle to articulate their goals, and how have you overcome them?
4. How do you balance providing structure with allowing flexibility in the coachee's goal-setting process?
5. In what ways can you further integrate the SMART framework into your coaching practice to support more effective goal achievement?

Chapter 7
Developing coaching skills: the art of connection, listening and powerful questioning in great coaching

This chapter is your gateway to understanding the essential elements that make a coach truly exceptional. We will start by examining what sets a great coach apart and the core beliefs that underpin their effectiveness. These foundational beliefs are not just abstract concepts; they are the driving force behind successful coaching practices.

As we explore the art of connection, active listening and powerful questioning, you will see how these skills are deeply intertwined with the principles of great coaching. By understanding the beliefs that guide exceptional coaches, you will gain insight into how these core skills are developed and refined. This chapter will demonstrate how a solid grasp of these beliefs enhances your ability to connect meaningfully with your coachees and ask questions that lead to profound insights.

Let's explore how these foundational beliefs shape practical skills that can elevate your coaching practice and lead to meaningful, transformative experiences for you and your coachees.

What makes a great coach?

At its core, great coaching is really about connection, empathy and a genuine desire to support someone else's growth. It is more than just knowing the right questions to ask or having a solid framework to follow; it is about being fully present with the person in front of you and creating a space where they feel seen, heard and valued.

Carl Rogers revolutionised the way we think about coaching, transforming leadership, management and personal development in the 1980s. His groundbreaking work introduced the idea that coaching is not a one-size-fits-all process but rather exists on a spectrum. At one end of this spectrum is a more directive approach, where the coach listens, offers advice and provides guidance when needed. While this may not align with the purest form of coaching, it still draws on fundamental coaching skills. As we move further along the spectrum, coaching shifts towards a non-directive approach, where the focus is less on giving direction and more on facilitating the coachee's own self-discovery and growth. Here, the coach's role is to ask questions that prompt the coachee to explore their thoughts and feelings more deeply, without imposing their own judgements or solutions. It is about helping the coachee find their own path, in their own time. What makes this spectrum approach so powerful is its adaptability, allowing coaching to be effective across so many different contexts.

Underpinning coaching beliefs

At the core of every effective coaching relationship are the beliefs that guide the process – beliefs that shape how we, as coaches, approach each conversation and interaction. These underlying principles form the foundation for creating a space where coachees can explore, grow and achieve meaningful change. Coaching is not just about helping people reach goals; it is about helping them unlock their potential by seeing the world in new ways and expanding the choices they have in front of them.

- One of the most essential coaching beliefs is that people are different from one another. Each of us has unique experiences, emotions and perceptions. We have created our own versions of reality based on what we have lived through. A great coach seeks to understand the world through the coachee's eyes. By recognising this, a coach can meet the coachee where they are, with genuine empathy and understanding.

- Another belief that sits at the heart of coaching is that we all have choices – about how we behave, what we think and how we feel. Coaching helps coachees explore these choices and expand them, opening up possibilities they may not have seen or thought about before. It is about helping people realise that, even in the toughest situations, there are always options available.

- An important truth in coaching is that people are always doing the best they can with the resources, awareness and experiences they currently have. No one is stagnant – there is always room for growth. Coaching is about helping coachees become more aware, more resourceful and more open to new experiences that enhance their ability to navigate life's challenges.

- Perhaps the most hopeful belief of all: change is possible. Coaching exists because people can grow, shift their mindsets and adopt new behaviours. However, change doesn't happen without first acknowledging the present reality. Coachees must be willing to face their current reality, and often this means working through their blind spots – those areas they may not even realise are holding them back. A coach helps shine a light on these blind spots, making the path forward clearer.
- A central tenet of coaching is that we already have the resources within us to create change. The coach's role is to help the coachee tap into those internal resources – the strengths, insights and abilities they may not fully recognise. Through thoughtful questions and reflection, a coach can guide the coachee to discover the power that lies within.
- Finally, one of the most empowering beliefs in coaching is that the coachee has the answers and the coach has the questions. The coach's job is not to provide solutions, but instead to ask the questions that help the coachee discover the answers for themselves. This belief shifts the dynamic from dependency to empowerment, allowing coachees to realise they have everything they need to move forward with confidence.

By grounding coaching in these core beliefs, we create an environment where coachees feel supported, empowered and capable of achieving real, lasting change. To be truly effective as a coach, you need a whole toolkit of skills that complement each other and help you support those you're coaching. Here are some practical strategies to help you develop these essential coaching skills.

The power of active listening

When I think about what it really takes to become a skilled coach, the first thing that comes to mind is active listening. It is such a simple concept on the surface – just listen. But when you dig deeper, you realise that truly listening to someone, without interruption or judgement, is an art form. It is about being fully present in the moment, giving the speaker your undivided attention, and creating a space where they feel heard and valued.

This kind of listening is not just about hearing words; it is about understanding the emotions and intentions behind those words. Looking back at my experiences with coaching, I am struck by just how important listening is. For all children and young people, being given time and attention is crucial. They need space to process their thoughts at their own pace. Rushing them doesn't just make them uncomfortable; it can lead to misunderstandings about their abilities. When we allow them the time to think and express themselves, we are not just being patient, we are showing that we value their unique way of thinking. Encouraging individuals, especially young people, to think for themselves is a core part of coaching. It is about validating their thought processes, helping them see that their way of understanding the world is valuable. This reduces the pressure to conform to a single way of thinking and allows them to embrace their unique perspectives.

> **Practical strategies**
> **Active listening**
> - You don't need much – just a partner, a quiet space and five minutes. One of you will speak and the other will listen. But here's the challenge: the listener doesn't speak, doesn't interrupt, doesn't judge. Instead, they focus entirely on the speaker, using non-verbal cues like eye contact and nodding to show they're engaged. This is not just about being polite; it is about creating a safe, supportive atmosphere where the speaker feels comfortable sharing.
> - After the exercise, take a moment to reflect on the experience.
>   - How did it feel to listen without speaking?
>   - How did it feel to be listened to without interruption?
> - This simple practice can be eye opening, revealing just how powerful and rare true listening is.

Powerful questioning

Questioning is another powerful tool in the coaching toolkit, and it is one that evolves significantly as you gain experience. At first, it is easy to fall into asking directive questions but, as you practise, you start to see the value in open-ended, reflective questions that prompt more thoughtful responses. For example, one of the teachers who spoke to me when I was researching for this book shared his realisation about his use of questions. He worked out that many of his questions were too closed, often leading students to guess what he wanted them to say rather than think for themselves. By shifting to more open questions, he encouraged his students to engage more deeply with the material.

Another teacher shared her experiences of how she learned to use language strategically in her questions. By adding a simple word like 'yet', she transformed a statement about not achieving a goal into a challenge to keep trying: 'You haven't managed to leave for home at 3.30 yet. How could you make that happen next time?' This subtle shift not only encourages persistence but also helps students to see challenges as opportunities for growth.

> ### Practical strategies
> **Powerful questioning**
> - Practise crafting open-ended questions that encourage deeper reflection.
> - Focus on questions that start with 'what' or 'how' rather than 'why', as they tend to invite more thoughtful responses without putting the person on the defensive. For example, instead of asking, 'Why did you make that decision?' (which might come across as judgemental or probing), ask, 'What factors influenced your decision?' This approach invites the person to explore their thought process and share insights without feeling defensive.
> - Try having a conversation where you only ask questions, while the other person responds to them. It is a great way to shift the focus from providing answers to facilitating self-discovery.

Building rapport

Building rapport is about establishing a strong foundation of trust, respect and genuine connection, which makes the coaching process more effective and impactful. Rapport acts as a bridge that helps coachees feel safe, valued and understood, creating an environment where they are more willing to open up and engage deeply.

When coachees experience this connection, they are not only more comfortable sharing their thoughts, feelings and challenges, they are also more receptive to feedback and reflection. This trust allows the coach to ask more challenging questions, facilitating deeper exploration and growth.

Strong rapport also empowers coachees to take risks, embrace vulnerability and be honest in their self-assessment – all crucial for meaningful progress in their coaching journey. Ultimately, building rapport is the cornerstone of a successful coaching relationship, enabling transformative conversations that lead to lasting change.

Practical strategies
Building rapport
- Spend time with someone, focusing on establishing a genuine connection. Mirror their body language and tone, to build trust and comfort.
- Be fully present, show interest in their stories and share your own relevant experiences, to strengthen the relationship.
- Ask open-ended questions and listen actively to demonstrate genuine curiosity and empathy. This encourages the other person to share more deeply, and fosters a sense of mutual understanding and connection.

Staying in the not knowing

As a coach, staying in the 'not knowing' is one of the most powerful and essential aspects of the coaching process. It enables the coach to remain open, curious and fully present with the coachee, rather than rushing to offer solutions or projecting personal assumptions. By embracing the 'not knowing', the coach invites deeper exploration, giving the coachee the space to reflect, gain insights and discover their own answers.

This approach fosters true empowerment, shifting the focus from the coach as the expert to the coachee as the expert in their own experience. By resisting the urge to direct or control the conversation, the coach creates a more authentic and reflective process, allowing for transformative growth. Ultimately, staying in the 'not knowing' builds a trusting, collaborative relationship that encourages both vulnerability and strength in the coaching dialogue.

Practical strategies
Staying in the not knowing
- Engage in a coaching practice session where your goal is to withhold advice and solutions. This exercise helps you focus on fostering coachee self-discovery rather than directing the conversation.
- Prioritise asking open-ended questions that prompt the coachee to delve deeply into their thoughts and experiences. Use questions such as, 'What do you think is behind this feeling?' or 'What opportunities might this situation present?' to stimulate meaningful reflection.

- Allow the coachee to lead the exploration by refraining from steering the conversation towards specific outcomes. This approach encourages them to take ownership of their insights and decisions.
- Practise deliberate pauses during the coaching session before responding to the coachee. This technique helps you resist the urge to immediately provide answers, creating more space for the coachee to think and reflect.
- Reflect on the impact of staying in the pause by assessing how it influences the depth and quality of the conversation.
- Notice how giving the coachee time to process before you respond can enhance their engagement and self-discovery.

Managing silence

Silence is often an underappreciated but highly effective tool in coaching. When used intentionally, it creates space for reflection and deeper thinking, allowing the coachee to process their thoughts and emotions at their own pace. Rather than feeling the need to fill every moment with conversation, embracing silence can lead to more meaningful insights.

By becoming comfortable with these pauses, you foster an environment where the coachee feels safe to explore their ideas more fully, consider different perspectives and arrive at their own conclusions. Silence can also signal to the coachee that you trust their ability to find solutions, empowering them to take ownership of their development. In this way, managing silence is not about withholding input, but about creating the right conditions for personal growth and thoughtful self-discovery.

Practical strategies
Managing silence
- Practise sitting in silence: After asking a deep question, remain silent to give the other person time to think and formulate their response. Use this exercise to become comfortable with silence, which can often lead to more profound insights and reflections.
- Observe and note the impact of silence: During your practice, reflect on how the use of silence affects the coaching session. Consider how it influences the depth of responses, and how it can encourage the other person to engage in more thoughtful and meaningful reflection.

- Use silence strategically: Implement silence intentionally in your coaching sessions to prompt deeper thought. Plan moments of silence after key questions or significant revelations, to allow for greater introspection and clarity.
- Evaluate your comfort with silence: Regularly assess how comfortable you are with silence and identify any discomfort you may feel. Work on building your tolerance to use silence effectively as a tool to enhance the coaching process.

Summarising

Summarising is a powerful technique in coaching that helps ensure clarity and mutual understanding between coach and coachee. By using phrases like, 'What I'm hearing is …' or 'It sounds like you're saying …', the coach reflects the key points of what the coachee has shared. This not only confirms that the coach has accurately understood their thoughts and feelings but also gives the coachee an opportunity to hear their own words framed slightly differently, which can lead to deeper insight or new perspectives.

Summarising allows the conversation to stay focused, helps highlight important themes and reinforces that the coachee's voice is being heard, ultimately creating a space for more meaningful reflection and growth.

Practical strategies
Summarising

- Reflect back key points: After listening to a partner share a challenge, summarise the main ideas by using phrases such as, 'What I am hearing is …' or 'So, it sounds like …' to capture and confirm your understanding of their perspective.
- Encourage confirmation and feedback: Ask the partner to review your summary for accuracy with questions like, 'Does this capture what you were trying to express?' or 'Is there anything I missed or misunderstood?' This helps refine your summarising skills and ensures clarity.
- Practise active listening: Focus on what is being said and on the underlying emotions and themes. Use these insights to create a more accurate and empathetic summary that reflects both content and context.

- Provide concise summaries: Aim to distil information into clear, concise statements that highlight the essence of the conversation. Avoid overloading with details and focus on capturing the core message.
- Use summarising to validate understanding: Incorporate summarising as a tool to validate your comprehension throughout the conversation. Regularly check in by summarising key points and asking for feedback to ensure ongoing mutual understanding.
- Develop summarising habits: Make summarising a habitual part of your coaching sessions. Practise summarising at different stages of the conversation to reinforce important points and maintain focus on the coachee's key issues and goals.

Paraphrasing

Paraphrasing involves restating what the coachee has just said, using slightly different words while maintaining the original meaning. It is an active listening technique that shows the coachee they have been heard and understood. Paraphrasing focuses on reflecting back specific points or emotions the coachee has shared, often in shorter snippets.

This technique helps the coachee hear their own thoughts from a fresh perspective, often revealing deeper insights or clarifying emotions that were not immediately obvious. For instance, if a coachee says, 'I feel overwhelmed with all my responsibilities at work', the coach might paraphrase by saying, 'It sounds like you are feeling a lot of pressure from the number of tasks on your plate.' The subtle shift in language can provide the coachee with a moment of reflection, allowing them to confirm or correct the coach's understanding.

Practical strategies
Paraphrasing
- Pair up for practise: Team up with a colleague. Have one person share a current challenge or situation while the other practises paraphrasing the key points and underlying emotions expressed.
- Role reversal: After 10 minutes, switch roles so that each person has the opportunity to both share and paraphrase. This allows you to practise the skill from both perspectives and gain fuller understanding of its impact.

- Reflect on the process: After completing the exercise, discuss how paraphrasing influences the conversation. Focus on whether it helped the coachee feel heard and understood, and how it contributed to gaining clarity on the challenge.
- Evaluate effectiveness: Use questions like, 'Did the paraphrasing capture the essence of what you were trying to convey?' and 'How did it impact your sense of being understood?' to gauge the effectiveness of your paraphrasing.
- Identify areas for improvement: Discuss any challenges encountered during the exercise, such as difficulties in capturing emotions or missing key points. Use this feedback to refine and enhance your paraphrasing skills.
- Practise regularly: Incorporate paraphrasing exercises into your regular practise routine to build confidence and proficiency. The more you practise, the more naturally the skill will integrate into your coaching conversations.

Reflective practice

Reflective practice is a powerful tool for continuous improvement, especially in coaching. By regularly reflecting on your coaching experiences, you gain deeper insights into your strengths, areas for growth and the impact of your interactions with coachees. This process allows you to critically evaluate your approach, identifying patterns in your behaviour, communication and decision-making.

Practical strategies

Reflective practice

- Post-session reflection: Immediately after each coaching session, set aside time to reflect on the experience. Consider what went well, what could have been improved, and any notable moments. Document your reflections in a journal to track patterns and identify areas for growth over time.
- Journaling practise: Regularly review your journal entries to spot recurring themes, challenges or successful strategies. This practice helps you gain insights into your coaching style and effectiveness, guiding your ongoing development.

- Engage in peer coaching: Partner with a colleague or fellow coach to engage in peer coaching. Take turns coaching each other on specific issues or challenges, then spend time reflecting together on the experience.
- Reflective discussion: After each peer coaching session, discuss with your partner what you learned from the exercise. Focus on both your own and your partner's performance, and explore insights gained about your coaching approach and areas for improvement.
- Identify actionable insights: Use the feedback from peer coaching to identify specific actions or changes you can implement in your practice. This collaborative reflection helps you refine your skills and approach based on diverse perspectives.
- Incorporate feedback: Regularly seek and incorporate feedback from your coachees, peers or supervisors. Use their input to enhance your reflective practice and adjust your coaching strategies accordingly.

Giving and receiving feedback

Feedback is vital for growth, both for the coachee and the coach. As coaches, it's important to provide feedback that is constructive and empowering, highlighting the coachee's strengths while guiding them towards areas of improvement.

Equally essential is being open to receiving feedback from the coachee, fostering a culture of mutual respect and collaboration. This two-way dialogue not only enhances the coaching relationship but also models how feedback can be a powerful tool for continuous learning and development, deepening trust and encouraging meaningful progress.

Practical strategies
Giving and receiving feedback
- Provide constructive feedback: Engage in an exercise where you offer feedback to a peer. Ensure your feedback is clear, specific and balanced, focusing on both strategies and areas for improvement. Use examples to illustrate your points, and maintain a supportive tone.
- Receive feedback graciously: After providing feedback, receive feedback from your peer. Practise active listening by refraining from interrupting or becoming defensive. Fully absorb the feedback and take time to reflect on its content.

- Reflect on feedback: Consider how the feedback can inform your personal and professional growth. Identify actionable steps you can take based on the insights shared.
- Ask clarifying questions: If any part of the feedback is unclear, ask thoughtful questions to gain a deeper understanding. This shows your commitment to improvement and helps ensure you correctly interpret the feedback.
- Share feedback experiences: After the exercise, discuss with your peer how the feedback process felt from both perspectives. Reflect on what aspects were helpful and what could be improved for future feedback exchanges.
- Incorporate feedback into practice: Use the feedback to make specific changes in your approach or behaviour. Track your progress over time to see how the feedback has impacted your performance and development.
- Regular feedback practice: Make feedback a regular part of your practice by scheduling ongoing sessions with peers or mentors. Regular feedback helps maintain continuous improvement and reinforces a culture of openness and growth.

Coaching is about more than just developing skills; it's about creating an environment where those skills can flourish. Whether it's through active listening, powerful questioning or building rapport, the goal is to support the growth and transformation of those you coach. By practising these techniques regularly, you'll not only become a more effective coach but also contribute to a more supportive, inclusive and dynamic learning environment.

In the end, coaching isn't just about helping others – it's about growing alongside them. As you develop your skills, you'll find that the lessons you learn in coaching have a way of spilling over into other areas of your life, making you a better listener, communicator and leader.

Summary

- Coaching skills such as connection, empathy and active listening are emphasised as core components of effective coaching.
- Carl Rogers' approach is referenced to illustrate the coaching spectrum, from a directive style to a more non-directive, reflective approach that supports the coachee's self-discovery.
- Active listening is explored as a foundational skill, requiring the coach to be fully present and create a space where the coachee feels truly seen and heard.
- Powerful questioning and rapport building are highlighted as essential techniques in fostering a strong coach–coachee relationship.
- Managing silence, summarising and engaging in reflective practice are discussed as important tools for effective coaching conversations.
- Giving and receiving feedback is outlined as a valuable part of the coaching process, helping both coach and coachee to grow.
- Exercises are provided to help coaches strengthen their skills, promoting a coaching environment that supports the growth and transformation of both coach and coachee.

Reflection questions

1. How can you improve your active listening skills to better understand the emotions behind the words your coachee shares?
2. In what ways could you incorporate more open-ended, reflective questions into your coaching practice to encourage deeper thinking?
3. How does silence play a role in your coaching sessions, and how might embracing it more fully enhance your coachee's self-reflection?
4. How comfortable are you with giving and receiving feedback in coaching? What steps could you take to make feedback more constructive and empowering?
5. After a coaching session, how do you reflect on your own practice? What insights have emerged from your reflections that could improve future sessions?

Chapter 8
Time to think: the transformative power of reflection

In the fast-paced environment of schools, where every moment is accounted for, finding time to think deeply is a rare commodity. Coaching provides a unique opportunity for educators to carve out that much-needed reflective space. Many teachers describe their coaching experiences as moments of profound self-discovery and reflection.

One of the teachers who spoke to me when I was researching this book captured this sentiment perfectly. She expressed how coaching allowed her to reconnect with her values, stating, 'It gave me the space to listen to myself, to understand what I truly needed to focus on, and to realign my priorities in both my personal and professional life'.

For many educators, this reflective space becomes a vital tool for navigating the complexities of teaching. It provides them with the time and mental space to identify and challenge limiting beliefs, develop new perspectives and, ultimately, grow in ways that extend far beyond the classroom. The ripple effects of this growth can be seen in their relationships with students, the culture within the school and the overall sense of job satisfaction.

In a profession that often emphasises the needs of others, coaching shifts the focus back to the individual teacher – encouraging personal growth and resilience. This reflective process can be transformative, equipping educators with the tools to not only navigate the pressures of the school environment but to thrive within it, fostering their own flourishing as well as that of their students.

The elusive nature of time in schools

The elusive nature of time in schools is a constant challenge faced by educators. Time is often the most discussed, yet most elusive, resource. Teachers and school leaders alike are continuously grappling with how to manage their limited time effectively, especially amid the overwhelming priorities, deadlines and ever-growing number of initiatives that fill the school calendar. The pressure to meet these demands leaves little room for reflection, planning or professional development, leading to a sense of perpetual scarcity when it comes to time.

Anthony and van Nieuwerburgh's (2018) study sheds light on a key challenge, revealing that a perceived 'lack of time' is one of the greatest obstacles to implementing coaching initiatives in schools. Despite the acknowledged long-term benefits of coaching, it is frequently seen as an extra burden in an already overextended profession.

This concern was echoed by the teachers I spoke with, who initially feared that coaching would demand too much time: 'I thought coaching would take an awful lot of setting up … but it really didn't; it just took a little bit of thought.'

Once engaged in the process, many realised that coaching, rather than draining time, optimised it by fostering clearer thinking and better decision-making.

This paradox of time and coaching is perhaps best addressed by Nancy Kline (1999), who advocates for the intentional creation of time to think – what she refers to as a 'thinking environment'. Kline argues that such spaces are increasingly rare in our modern, fast-paced world, noting, 'It has been squeezed out of our lives and organisations by inferior ways of treating each other. Organisations, families, and relationships can become "Thinking Environments" again, where good ideas abound, action follows, and people flourish' (p. 13). Schools can benefit from reclaiming time for deep reflection and meaningful dialogue. When structured properly, coaching provides a space for exactly this – a moment to pause, reflect and refocus during a hectic school day.

By embedding coaching into the rhythm of school life and reframing it not as an additional task, but as a tool to enhance effectiveness, schools can begin to address the elusive nature of time. Instead of seeing coaching as another commitment on an already full plate, it becomes a mechanism to streamline thinking, prioritise actions and align daily tasks with long-term goals. Teachers, too, can experience a shift in how they view time – not as something that constantly slips away, but as a resource that can be harnessed to improve not only their own practice, but also student outcomes.

The challenge, then, is not just about finding time, but about making time valuable. Schools that embrace coaching as part of their culture can create environments where time is used more effectively. By creating these 'thinking environments', schools can move from reactive, rushed environments to proactive spaces of collaboration, reflection and thoughtful action. This cultural shift not only improves the quality of decisions but also supports the wellbeing of both teachers and students. In an educational landscape that constantly demands more, creating space for coaching and reflective practice is one of the most powerful investments a school can make in reclaiming and optimising its most elusive resource – time.

The power of structured reflection

Coaching is a practice deeply rooted in the present, focusing on an individual's goals and how they wish to achieve them. For coaching to be successful, it must promote deep reflection and foster meaningful change. Teachers often describe the deeper level of thinking that occurs during coaching sessions, which mirrors the concepts found in Kline's 'thinking environments'. These environments create the right conditions for individuals to work through different levels and states of change.

My own coaching practices have been heavily influenced by Kline's work, particularly her identification of key components necessary to support a person's best thinking. These principles can be adapted to various situations and profoundly affect how we conduct conversations, whether one-to-one or in larger groups.

Nancy Kline's 10 key components to support a person's best thinking, as part of her Time to Think methodology are:

1. **Attention** – Listening with full focus and without interruption.
2. **Equality** – Treating each other as equals, valuing each person's voice equally.
3. **Ease** – Creating a relaxed environment, free from pressure or urgency.
4. **Appreciation** – Regularly affirming and acknowledging the positive aspects of the person and their thinking.
5. **Encouragement** – Encouraging people to think for themselves and take risks in their thinking, without fear of judgement.
6. **Feelings** – Allowing and addressing feelings so they don't block thinking.
7. **Information** – Providing all necessary information to help the person think clearly and make decisions.
8. **Diversity** – Embracing and integrating different perspectives and ways of thinking.
9. **Incisive questions** – Asking thought-provoking, challenging questions that remove limiting assumptions.

10. **Place** – Creating a physical environment that is conducive to thinking, where the person feels comfortable and safe.

I have implemented these concepts in my workplaces by restructuring meetings to include dedicated thinking time for all participants, rather than just listing agenda items. This approach has positively impacted the outcomes of meetings, laying a solid foundation for introducing a coaching culture. The agenda is shared with teachers a few days in advance, giving them time to reflect and prepare thoughtful responses. During the meeting, we establish a speaking order so that everyone knows they will have an opportunity to contribute. Each person is allocated five minutes per agenda item and we set a clear ground rule of no interruptions, ensuring that everyone is heard and listened to attentively. This approach keeps the meeting solution-focused, encourages collaboration, and ensures that the next steps are both clear and actionable. To close each meeting, we take time to appreciate and acknowledge one another's strengths, fostering a sense of respect and positive reinforcement, which further strengthens our collaborative culture and commitment to shared goals.

An example of a teacher meeting agenda

Agenda item	Questions
Student engagement strategies	What methods have you found most successful in engaging students? How can we adapt our current strategies to better meet the diverse needs of our students?
Curriculum review and alignment	How well do our current teaching materials align with the learning outcomes we have set for this term? Where do we see gaps in the curriculum and what resources do we need to address them?
Professional development opportunities	What areas of professional growth would you like to focus on in the coming term? How can we make time and resources available to ensure all staff benefit from professional development?
Parental involvement and communication	What communication strategies have worked well for engaging parents in their child's journey? How can we create more opportunities for parents to be involved in supporting classroom activities or school events?

Creating a thinking environment in the classroom

In a classroom setting, a 'thinking environment' is one where both students and teachers are empowered to ask questions, explore ideas and engage in respectful dialogue. This is closely aligned with coaching practices, where the goal is to create a space that encourages curiosity, open expression and reflection. Just as a coach fosters a safe, non-judgemental environment for their coachee to think deeply and explore ideas, a thinking environment in the classroom invites students to share their thoughts without fear of criticism. By encouraging this openness, teachers act as facilitators of learning, helping students to develop critical thinking skills, independence, and confidence in their ability to generate and express ideas. This coach-like practice ultimately promotes deeper learning, emotional intelligence and a sense of ownership over the learning process.

A teacher might ask a student, 'What do you think this means?' and then give the student time to think before expecting a response. This pause, although small, signals to the student that their thoughts are valued, and that careful reflection is more important than rushing to answer. Much like in a coaching session, this pause creates space for deeper thinking and encourages the student to engage in meaningful self-reflection. In this way, the teacher is using a coach-like approach, allowing the student to take ownership of their learning process.

Below, I have shared some strategies that can help cultivate this kind of thinking environment, where thoughtful dialogue and exploration are prioritised over quick answers.

Practical strategies
Build a culture of equality

- Establish clear classroom norms that encourage equal participation. Make it a practice to call on quieter students as well as more vocal ones, ensuring that all students' voices are heard.
- Use a 'speaking token' or similar tool during group discussions to ensure that everyone has an opportunity to speak without interruption.
- When students feel that their ideas are valued equally, they are more likely to engage and share their thoughts, fostering an environment of intellectual risk-taking and collaboration.

Give time to think
- After posing a question, give students 10–15 seconds of silence to think before expecting responses. Use 'think–pair–share' to allow them to first discuss their ideas with a partner before sharing with the class.
- After asking, 'How does this connect with what we learned yesterday?', ask students to jot down their thoughts quietly for one minute before discussing.
- Students feel less pressure to answer immediately, which can lead to deeper, more thoughtful responses. This strategy normalises silence as a part of the thinking process.

Ask open-ended, thought-provoking questions
- Frame questions that encourage deeper thinking and multiple perspectives. Avoid yes/no or simple recall questions. Use prompts such as, 'What if ...?' or 'How might ...?' to push students beyond surface-level responses.
- Instead of asking, 'What is the main theme of this story?' ask, 'How might the story change if it was told from another character's perspective?'
- Open-ended questions inspire curiosity and critical thinking, allowing students to explore ideas more fully and creatively.

Practise active listening
- Model active listening by paraphrasing what students have said before responding, demonstrating that their ideas are being heard and considered.
- If a student says, 'I think the character feels trapped', the teacher might respond, 'It sounds like you believe the character's choices are limited – can you explain more about why you feel that way?'
- This builds trust and encourages students to elaborate on their thoughts, knowing their contributions are respected.

Create trust and safety
- Establish ground rules that promote mutual respect, such as no interruptions during individual responses and the use of constructive language in discussions.
- At the start of the year, co-create a classroom agreement with students that emphasises listening respectfully, taking turns and offering supportive feedback.

- When students feel safe from ridicule or judgement, they are more willing to express new ideas and engage in critical thinking.

Normalise reflection and self-correction
- Allow students the opportunity to revise or build upon their answers after hearing others speak. Let them know that it is okay to change their minds as they gather more information.
- After a discussion, say, 'Does anyone want to add to or change their original thought after hearing other perspectives?'
- This encourages students to think flexibly and see learning as an evolving process rather than one fixed on immediate, perfect answers.

Utilise non-verbal cues and body language
- Use body language such as nodding, maintaining eye contact, and open postures to show that you are engaged in the student's response, even when they are still formulating their thoughts.
- If a student is struggling to articulate an answer, the teacher might lean forward slightly, offering quiet encouragement through non-verbal cues, giving the student confidence to continue.
- Non-verbal support can provide reassurance, especially for students who may be less confident in sharing their thoughts.

Integrate reflection time
- Build moments of reflection into the lesson where students can process and organise their thoughts before sharing.
- At the end of a discussion, ask students to write down one thing they learned and one question they still have. Allow time for quiet reflection before discussing the next steps.
- Reflection time gives students the space to internalise learning, helping them engage more deeply in future discussions.

Encourage peer-to-peer dialogue
- Use pair or small group discussions to allow students to practise articulating their thoughts in a lower-pressure environment before sharing with the class.
- Before a full-class discussion, ask students to turn to a partner and discuss their initial responses to a question like, 'Why do you think the character made that decision?'
- Students often feel more comfortable exploring ideas with peers first, which helps build confidence for larger discussions.

> **Celebrate ideas and growth**
> - Regularly acknowledge students' ideas and contributions, focusing on their thought processes rather than just correct answers.
> - At the end of a discussion, highlight diverse ideas shared by students, such as, 'I appreciated how Maya connected the story to her own life experience, and how Sam offered a different perspective on the character's motivations.'
> - Recognising the value of different viewpoints encourages continued participation and builds a sense of intellectual community in the classroom.

Ultimately, creating a thinking environment in the classroom is about more than just facilitating discussions – it's about building a culture where every student feels valued, respected and empowered to think deeply. These practical strategies can help teachers foster an environment that encourages critical thinking, collaboration and continuous growth. When students feel safe to share their ideas, engage in meaningful reflection and take intellectual risks, they not only learn more effectively but also develop a lifelong love of learning.

The power of time to think

Giving people the time to think can be incredibly transformative. One of the teacher-coaches I spoke to shared their experience of this process, saying, 'I believe it's very powerful to give people some thinking time that they don't usually have, and I believe that coaching can really impact their "mobility of thinking". I witness it time and time again – you just watch the penny drop.'

This reflection highlights how providing space for deep thought can lead to clarity and new insights, as individuals find solutions that might otherwise remain obscured by the rush of daily tasks.

Another educator, who provides coaching across schools, described how coaching and creating time to think reshaped the culture in one of the schools he worked in:

I got a phone call from the school saying they'd like to organise some coaching within the school. They'd been thinking about it and talking about it, and asked if I be willing to go in to do some coaching? Initially, they wanted me to coach middle leaders – teachers who had additional responsibilities – to support them in their new roles. They thought that by bringing me in, they would have someone to go to if they had issues or struggles or were feeling stressed by anything. They would have someone outside of the leadership team to turn to.

This story shows how the power of coaching and thinking time helps educators reflect, problem-solve and grow. By creating space for middle leaders to step back from their demanding roles and think, the school fostered a culture where staff could deeply reflect on challenges and find meaningful solutions. This structured time, dedicated to reflection through coaching, allowed leaders to build confidence, improve decision-making and enhance their effectiveness.

Practical strategies

Structured reflection time

- Dedicate specific time slots in the school week to engage in reflection. This could be through coaching sessions, staff development meetings or even personal reflection periods.
- Introduce 15-minute 'thinking blocks' after staff meetings or at the start of planning sessions, where teachers are encouraged to reflect on challenges, brainstorm solutions or think through upcoming tasks without distractions.
- Create dedicated space to reflect on their practices, leading to more strategic planning and problem-solving.

Regular coaching check-ins

- Integrate short, regular coaching sessions (even 20–30 minutes is enough) into the school schedule to allow staff time to think through challenges and refine their goals.
- Set up monthly coaching cycles for middle leaders or teachers who may be facing new challenges. These sessions should focus on providing space for the individual to reflect on their goals, priorities and any challenges they face.
- Regular check-ins provide a consistent structure for reflection, helping move from reacting to daily stressors to proactively addressing long-term goals and development.

Mindful pause before decision-making

- Encourage staff to take a mindful pause before making important decisions. This allows time to assess the situation clearly before reacting.

- In meetings or during busy times, establish the habit of asking, 'Let's take a moment to think about this before we decide.' Even short pauses of 30 seconds can lead to clearer, more thoughtful decisions.
- A mindful pause can prevent reactive decision-making and ensure more considered responses, especially in high-pressure environments.

Peer reflection groups

- Set up small peer reflection groups with other teachers so you can regularly meet to share experiences, ask questions and reflect on your teaching practices.
- Create cross-departmental groups that meet every few weeks to discuss their challenges and offer each other insights. Encourage reflective questioning and listening, using coaching techniques like active listening and paraphrasing.
- Peer groups offer a collaborative space for reflection, where teachers can learn from one another's experiences and gain new perspectives on their own challenges.

Thinking environment in staff meetings

- Incorporate Nancy Kline's 'thinking environment' principles into staff meetings by allowing moments of silence and reflection after key questions or discussions.
- After presenting an issue or decision, allow staff a few moments of quiet thinking time before inviting responses. This simple pause allows deeper reflection and more thoughtful contributions.
- Meetings become more solution-focused, as participants are given time to consider their responses, leading to more productive discussions.

By offering a safe, non-judgemental space for educators to reflect on their practices, coaching not only alleviates stress but also supports strategic thinking. This leads to what – as we saw a little earlier – one teacher-coach described as 'mobility of thinking' – the ability to move beyond immediate concerns and explore longer-term solutions. When teachers and leaders are given the opportunity to slow down, reflect and engage in thoughtful conversations, they gain new perspectives, feel more empowered in their roles and create a ripple effect that positively impacts the entire school community. Embedding reflective practices and coaching into the fabric of school life is not just about providing time; it is about creating value in that time. By making time for reflection a priority, schools can cultivate a culture of innovation, wellbeing and resilience. It is a powerful investment in both personal and professional growth, which ultimately benefits both staff and students.

Wellbeing through reflection

Managing stress and complexity in the teaching profession requires more than just coping strategies – it calls for intentional spaces to reflect and recalibrate. Teaching is deeply rewarding, but it comes with its own unique challenges. Teachers constantly juggle emotional support for students, administrative tasks, curriculum demands and their own personal pressures. The weight of these responsibilities can easily become overwhelming, leading to burnout if not carefully managed. This is where reflection, facilitated through coaching, becomes not only a professional necessity but also a vital form of self-care. In a profession that demands constant giving, reflective practices provide teachers with an opportunity to pause, breathe and reconnect with their purpose. These moments of reflection allow teachers to step back from the whirlwind of daily tasks and take much-needed time to process their experiences.

However, this reflective space offers more than just a mental break. It allows teachers to engage in deeper, more meaningful reflection, acknowledging challenges, confronting frustrations and processing the emotional weight of their work. By taking the time to reflect, teachers can shift from merely surviving the day to actively engaging in their own growth. They develop strategies for managing their workload, addressing classroom dynamics and taking care of their own emotional wellbeing. Coaching plays a key role in guiding this reflective process, offering a structured yet flexible framework for teachers to explore their experiences in a non-judgemental space. Through coaching conversations, teachers gain clarity, not only about what is happening in their classrooms but also about how they are feeling, reacting and adapting to these challenges. These conversations help teachers identify patterns, celebrate small wins and create actionable steps for moving forward.

In the long term, regular reflection is not just a way to manage stress; it's an investment in the teacher's overall wellbeing. Teachers who consistently engage in reflective practices are often better equipped to navigate the complexities of their role, regaining a sense of control, perspective and purpose. In doing so, they enhance both their own wellbeing and their effectiveness in the classroom, benefiting their students and the wider school community.

Practical strategies

Dedicated reflection time

- Schedule regular, dedicated time for reflection within the school week, such as 10-15 minutes at the end of each day or a longer session during professional development days.
- Create a quiet, comfortable space where you can sit with your thoughts. This could involve journaling about the day's challenges and successes or simply sitting in silence to process events. Consider prompts such as, 'What went well today?' or 'What would I like to improve for tomorrow?'
- Regular reflection time can help you acknowledge your daily efforts, release stress and prepare for the following day with a clearer mindset.

Coaching for emotional resilience

- Use coaching to support developing emotional resilience by exploring how you manage stress and your emotional reactions to challenges.
- In coaching sessions, focus on emotional wellbeing by asking questions like, 'How are you feeling about your workload?' or 'What emotions are you noticing when you face difficult classroom dynamics?' Encourage others to reflect on their emotional triggers and develop coping strategies to handle stress.
- Become more aware of your emotional responses and learn how to regulate them, leading to improved emotional resilience and overall wellbeing.

Reflection journals

- Keep reflection journals where you can regularly document your thoughts, challenges and emotional experiences.
- Use journal prompts like, 'What challenged me today, and how did I respond?' or 'What small wins did I achieve today?' Write freely about both positive experiences and difficulties.
- Journaling allows you to track your growth, recognise recurring patterns, and gain insights into your emotional and professional development over time.

Peer reflection groups

- Create peer reflection groups where you can meet regularly to discuss your challenges, share experiences and offer support.

- Set up small groups that meet once or twice a month, providing a structured space to reflect on your experiences. Use reflective questioning techniques such as, 'What have you learned about yourself in handling this challenge?' or 'What support do you need to move forward?'
- Peer reflection groups provide a sense of community and shared understanding, helping teachers feel supported while also encouraging collaborative problem-solving.

Guided meditation or mindfulness
- Integrate short, guided meditation or mindfulness exercises into the school day to help you and students to pause, reflect and reduce stress.
- Offer five- to ten-minute mindfulness sessions. Apps like Headspace and Calm can be useful tools. Focus on breathing or engage in a body scan to release tension and centre your thoughts.
- Mindfulness practices can help manage stress by bringing you into the present moment, reducing the mental and emotional clutter that builds up during the school day.

Post-lesson reflection
- Encourage teachers to reflect on their lessons immediately after teaching, focusing on what worked, what didn't and how they felt about the experience.
- Use simple reflection prompts like, 'What did I notice about my students' engagement today?' or 'How did I feel about the way I handled that challenge?' Teachers can jot down notes or discuss their reflections with a peer or coach.
- Post-lesson reflection helps teachers continuously refine their practice, and process any emotions or challenges they encountered, leading to professional growth and a clearer sense of direction.

Celebrating successes
- Incorporate regular moments for teachers to reflect on and celebrate their successes, however small they may seem.
- At the end of the week, ask teachers to share one thing they're proud of or something that went well. This can be done individually or as part of a group reflection session.
- Acknowledging successes helps shift the focus from stress and challenges to progress and achievements, boosting teachers' morale and reinforcing positive thinking.

Taking time to reflect is not just a luxury for teachers; it is essential to our wellbeing. By incorporating practical strategies like scheduled reflection time, coaching, journaling, peer support and mindfulness, schools can help teachers manage the stresses of their profession and rediscover their sense of purpose. Reflection allows teachers to process their experiences, gain clarity and develop actionable strategies to improve their practice. Ultimately, this investment in reflection strengthens not only the individual teacher but also the entire school community, creating a more supportive and effective educational environment.

Reflection as a catalyst for professional growth

Reflection is often associated with looking back, but its true power lies in its ability to propel us forward. In teaching, where demands are constant and often overwhelming, reflection becomes a crucial tool for growth and transformation. Through coaching, teachers are given the space to reflect and are guided to turn these reflections into actionable, future-oriented goals. When paired with coaching, reflection moves beyond simply reviewing past experiences; it becomes an active process of learning, planning and goal setting. Teachers begin to see their reflections as stepping stones, each offering valuable insights that inform their next steps. This shift from merely reflecting to actively shaping their future is one of the most empowering elements of coaching. It transforms teachers from passive recipients of change into active agents of their own growth.

What is most exciting about this forward-looking reflection is its ability to foster motivation and engagement. Teachers who regularly reflect and set actionable goals feel more invested in their journey. Instead of merely reacting to the daily demands of their profession, they take control. They set clear, meaningful goals and create pathways to achieve them – whether it is improving a specific teaching strategy, developing stronger relationships with students or working towards leadership roles within the school.

One teacher described the impact of learning how other teachers use coaching in their subjects as incredibly inspiring and wanted to bring that same energy to her own department. Another shared how coaching had reignited her passion for the job, while yet another reflected on how coaching had been transformative, using his experiences to develop leadership skills that helped create a culture of collaboration and healthy challenge within his school.

This proactive approach turns reflection into a dynamic driver of professional development. Teachers gain clarity on their strengths, identify areas for improvement and, most importantly, begin to view challenges as opportunities for growth. Over time, this process builds a deeper sense of agency, self-efficacy and resilience – qualities essential for sustaining long-term success and wellbeing in the teaching profession. In this way, reflection, particularly when supported by coaching, becomes a transformative practice. It keeps teachers engaged in their own learning, focused on their future, and empowered to shape their professional path with intention and purpose. Ultimately, this process benefits not only the individual teacher but also the students and school communities they serve.

Building a reflective culture

When teachers are given the time and space to reflect, they become more adaptable and innovative. Teaching is not a static profession; it requires constant evolution to meet the changing needs of students. Through regular reflection, educators can critically assess their methods, consider new approaches and adapt their practices to be more effective. This adaptability is key to creating responsive learning environments where students can thrive. Reflective practice also fosters a mindset of continuous improvement and creativity, encouraging teachers to view challenges as opportunities to experiment and innovate.

Reflection cultivates more than just adaptability; it nurtures creativity. Teachers who engage in reflective practice learn to view challenges not as roadblocks but as opportunities to experiment, innovate and find fresh solutions. Whether it's trying out new teaching strategies, integrating different technologies or rethinking classroom dynamics, reflective educators are better equipped to adapt to the demands of their students and the broader educational landscape. This creative flexibility keeps teaching dynamic and inspiring, benefiting both teachers and students alike.

The impact of reflection extends beyond individual growth. When reflective practice becomes a shared experience, it can shape the entire culture of a school. Teachers who regularly reflect and collaborate with colleagues foster a culture of openness, continuous learning and collective growth. In such a reflective school culture, educators support one another, freely sharing insights, challenges and successes. Reflection becomes a natural and integral part of the school's daily life, rather than a solitary or isolated exercise.

This kind of reflective culture does more than enhance individual teaching practices; it transforms the school into a collaborative, innovative environment where everyone is committed to improvement. Teachers who are part of such a culture feel supported in their professional journey, knowing that reflection isn't just encouraged but expected. The result is a stronger, more cohesive school community, where teachers, administrators and students alike benefit from a commitment to learning, growth and creativity. Ultimately, reflection – nurtured through both individual coaching and school-wide collaboration – creates a ripple effect that leads to lasting change. It fuels adaptation and innovation, driving improvements not only in the classroom but across the entire school community. By building a reflective culture, schools become places where both teachers and students can flourish, constantly evolving to meet new challenges with creativity, confidence and a shared sense of purpose. This collective commitment to reflection ensures that both individual and collective growth become cornerstones of the school's success, shaping a future of continuous improvement and empowerment for all.

Summary

- Time is often seen as an elusive resource in schools, with teachers and leaders struggling to find space for deep reflection amid daily demands.
- Creating intentional 'thinking time' can be transformative, allowing educators to step back, process experiences and gain clarity on challenges.
- Structured thinking time in coaching fosters deeper insights, encourages proactive problem-solving and shifts teachers from reactive to intentional action.
- Reflective coaching helps teachers reconnect with their purpose, enhances decision-making and builds resilience.
- Over time, dedicating time for reflection improves teacher wellbeing and contributes to a more collaborative, innovative school culture.
- Schools that prioritise thinking time for staff create environments where growth, creativity and wellbeing flourish, benefiting both teachers and students.

Reflection questions

1. How often do I consciously make time to reflect on my teaching practices, and what impact does this reflection have on my personal and professional growth?
2. In what ways can I create a 'thinking environment' in my classroom that encourages both my students and myself to engage in deeper, more meaningful reflection?

3. How do my current habits of listening and questioning during conversations influence the reflective space I provide for others? What changes might enhance this space?
4. What strategies can I implement to better manage the stress and complexity of my role as an educator through reflective practices?
5. How can I contribute to building a culture of reflection within my school, and what benefits might this bring to the broader school community?

Chapter 9
Emotional intelligence in coaching: the heart of the matter

Emotional intelligence really is the heart of great coaching. It is what allows us to tune in to our own emotions while staying in sync with what's going on emotionally for our coachees. This kind of awareness is key to creating a sense of psychological safety – a space where coachees feel comfortable enough to be open, honest and even vulnerable without worrying about being judged. When people feel safe, they are more willing to dive deep into their thoughts and emotions, which is where real growth happens. So, when we bring emotional intelligence into our coaching, we are not just building a stronger connection with our coachees; we're also helping them tackle challenges head on and make real progress. In the end, fostering this safe, emotionally aware environment is what makes our coaching truly impactful.

In this chapter, I want to dive into the profound impact of emotional intelligence in coaching, how it shapes the coaching relationship, and how we can cultivate and apply it in our practice.

The role of emotional intelligence in coaching

At its core, emotional intelligence is about being able to recognise, understand and manage our emotions while also being attuned to the emotions of others. Emotional intelligence is essential in coaching because it helps create a safe and supportive environment where coachees feel comfortable exploring their thoughts, feelings and behaviours. By fostering this sense of security, coaches enable deeper self-reflection and growth.

Let's break it down into some key components:

- Self-awareness: This is where it all begins. Understanding your own emotional triggers, strengths and limitations as a coach is crucial. Self-awareness helps you manage your responses and stay present with your coachee.

- Self-regulation: The ability to keep your emotions in check is vital. A calm, supportive coaching environment hinges on your ability to maintain composure, especially when your coachee is navigating intense emotions or complex issues.
- Empathy: This is the glue that connects you to your coachee. Empathy allows you to step into your coachee's shoes, to truly understand and share their feelings. When coachees feel understood, they feel valued, and that's when real progress happens.
- Social skills: Managing relationships effectively is key. In coaching, this means building rapport, communicating clearly and navigating the unique dynamics of the coach–coachee relationship.
- Motivation: A coach with high emotional intelligence is driven not just by outcomes but by a genuine investment in the coachee's growth and wellbeing. It's about being in their corner, cheering them on every step of the way.

Emotional intelligence allows us, as coaches, to create environments where clients feel seen, heard and supported. It opens the door to deeper, more meaningful conversations that go beyond surface-level issues, getting right to the heart of what drives and motivates them.

Cultivating emotional intelligence as a coach

Developing emotional intelligence is a continuous journey for both coaches and coachees. It begins with self-awareness – understanding our own emotional patterns, recognising how they shape our behaviours and interaction, and learning to manage them with intention. This self-awareness is the foundation of emotional intelligence and paves the way for building empathy, regulating emotions and creating deeper, more authentic coaching relationships. Below, I share some practical strategies to help you along this path.

Reflective practice

One of the most effective ways to develop emotional intelligence is through reflective practice.

Practical strategies

- Self-reflection on emotions: Regularly ask yourself reflective questions, such as:
  - How did my emotions influence my responses during the session?
  - Were there moments when my emotions overshadowed the needs of the coachee?
  - How did I manage my emotions in the moment?
- Coaching journal: Keep a coaching journal to document reflections on emotional responses during sessions. This helps track emotional patterns over time.
- Identifying emotional patterns: Use the journal to identify recurring emotional patterns, revealing areas for improvement in emotional intelligence, such as:
  - managing frustration
  - staying neutral during emotionally charged moments
  - navigating personal biases.
- Deepening emotional awareness: Engage in regular reflection to build greater awareness of your emotional landscape and its impact on the coaching dynamic.
- Strengthening emotional intelligence: Identify areas where emotional intelligence can be improved, focusing on emotional regulation, neutrality and awareness of biases.

By regularly engaging in reflection, you'll deepen your awareness of your emotional landscape and better understand how your emotions affect the coaching dynamic. Consider keeping a coaching journal where you document these reflections. Over time, patterns may emerge that reveal areas where your emotional intelligence can be strengthened, such as managing frustration, staying neutral in emotionally charged moments or navigating personal biases.

Mindfulness and presence

Mindfulness is an invaluable tool for staying present and emotionally grounded during coaching sessions. When you are fully present, you are better able to manage your emotions and keep the focus on your coachee's needs, rather than getting caught up in your own emotional reactions.

Practical strategies

- Daily mindfulness routine: Incorporate a short mindfulness practice into your daily routine. Start with five to ten minutes of meditation or deep breathing exercises each morning to train your focus and calm your mind.
- Pre-session centring: Before each coaching session, take two or three minutes to centre yourself. Sit quietly, close your eyes and focus on your breathing. This will help you enter the session feeling calm, present and fully attentive.
- Mindful listening: During the coaching session, practise active listening by focusing entirely on what your coachee is saying, without letting your mind wander. If distractions arise, gently redirect your attention back to your coachee's words.
- Pause before responding: When a coachee shares something challenging or emotional, pause for a moment before responding. This helps you avoid reacting impulsively, and ensures that your response is thoughtful and empathetic.
- Post-session reflection: After a coaching session, spend a few minutes reflecting on your mindfulness. Consider how well you stayed present, listened deeply and responded thoughtfully. Adjust your mindfulness practice as needed based on these reflections.
- Breathing anchor: Throughout the day, especially during moments of tension or uncertainty, return to your breath as an anchor. Take deep, slow breaths to centre yourself and calm your nervous system before responding to situations or challenges.

Empathy exercises

Empathy is central to emotional intelligence, as it allows you to truly understand and connect with your coachee's emotions. While some empathy comes naturally, it can also be developed through intentional practice. Here are a few exercises to enhance your empathy.

Practical strategies

- Role-playing practice: Set aside time to role-play with a peer or colleague. Take turns playing the roles of coach and coachee, focusing on stepping into the emotional and mental space of your coachee. After each role-playing session, reflect on the emotions and challenges experienced in the coachee role, discussing insights with your peer/colleague to deepen your understanding and empathetic responses.
- Active listening exercises: During conversations, focus entirely on the speaker without preparing your response while they speak. Use verbal and non-verbal cues like nodding or saying 'I see' to show you are engaged. After the speaker finishes, summarise what they have said to ensure understanding and show that you've truly listened. This reinforces empathy by acknowledging their emotions and thoughts.
- Daily perspective-taking: Throughout your day, make it a habit to actively imagine yourself in the shoes of others. Whether it is a colleague, friend or stranger, consider what they might be feeling or experiencing in that moment. Journal about these moments of perspective-taking, reflecting on what emotions or challenges you imagine others are facing, and how you can adjust your behaviour or responses to be more empathetic in the future.
- Emotion mapping: After coaching sessions, reflect on the emotions your coachee expressed and how they might have been feeling beneath their words. Write down possible emotional states (e.g. frustration, joy, confusion) and how you can address these feelings with empathy in future sessions.
- Empathy check-ins: Periodically ask trusted colleagues or peers for feedback on how empathetic you've been in your interactions. This outside perspective helps you refine and enhance your empathetic approach in both coaching and everyday conversations.

Incorporating these exercises into your routine not only sharpens your empathy skills but also deepens your ability to connect with your coachees in meaningful ways, ultimately fostering a more supportive coaching relationship.

Feedback seeking

Feedback is an essential part of developing emotional intelligence. Sometimes, we are not fully aware of how we come across emotionally to others, and hearing from those around us can provide valuable insights.

Practical strategies

- Ask your coachees or peers for feedback on your emotional presence during coaching sessions.
- Write down specific instances where your emotional presence either supported or hindered the conversation, and how you can adjust in future sessions.
- Ask yourself, 'How did my emotions influence the session?' and 'What specific actions can I take to improve emotional attunement?'
- Implement small adjustments immediately based on the feedback you receive. If a coachee mentions that you could be more emotionally responsive during a difficult conversation, make a conscious effort to acknowledge their emotions more explicitly in future sessions.
- Keep a personal journal after each session where you track your emotional presence, based on your own observations and feedback from coachees. This will help you become more mindful of your emotional state during coaching and track progress over time.
- In addition to seeking feedback from coachees, ask a coaching peer or supervisor to observe your sessions (if appropriate) and provide feedback on your emotional presence and responses. This external perspective can offer valuable insights for improvement.

See examples in my closing chapter and my link to further resources for coaching in education.

Continual learning

Emotional intelligence is a constantly evolving field, and staying curious is key to developing it over time.

Practical strategies

- Set time aside each week to read research articles, books or blogs on emotional intelligence, psychology and coaching. Create a list of credible sources (e.g. research journals or thought leaders) and subscribe to newsletters that regularly share the latest developments.
- Summarise key takeaways from the reading and reflect on how you can apply these insights to your coaching practice.
- Commit to attend at least one workshop, conference or seminar each year that focuses on emotional intelligence or coaching skills. Use these events to stay updated on new techniques and to network with professionals in the field.
- After attending, create an action plan outlining how you will incorporate new strategies into your coaching practice and share your learnings with peers or colleagues.
- Join a peer learning group or coaching circle where you can regularly discuss emotional intelligence and coaching topics. Share your own experiences and listen to other insights to broaden your perspective.
- Consider forming a group with colleagues if this doesn't yet exist in your area. Set monthly or bi-weekly meetings to explore emotional intelligence topics, case studies and practical applications.
- Enrol in online courses related to emotional intelligence, psychology or coaching. Many platforms offer certifications or specialisations in emotional intelligence, which can further enhance your knowledge and coaching expertise.
- Dedicate time each month to complete these courses and apply the techniques learned in your coaching sessions, keeping a log of what works best.
- Whenever you learn something new, whether from reading, a workshop or peer discussion, set aside time to reflect on how these insights can be integrated into your coaching approach. Write down practical applications and experiment with them in your sessions.
- Use journaling to track your progress, noting any changes in your coachees' responses and your own emotional intelligence growth.
- Find a mentor or a seasoned coach with a strong background in emotional intelligence. Meet with them regularly to discuss the latest trends, gain feedback on your learning journey and seek guidance on areas you want to improve.

As you continue to learn, you'll gain new tools and perspectives that can enhance your coaching practice. Consider setting aside time for professional development in emotional intelligence just as you would for other coaching competencies. Staying curious about your own emotional growth ensures that you remain an emotionally intelligent and effective coach.

Cultivating emotional intelligence is not a one-time effort but an ongoing process of reflection, mindfulness, empathy-building and learning. By committing to these practical steps, you will enhance your ability to connect with coachees, manage your emotions effectively, and create a coaching environment that promotes deep personal growth for both yourself and those you support. Emotional intelligence, when fully integrated into your coaching practice, helps you foster a trusting, supportive space where coachees feel empowered to explore, reflect and transform.

The impact of emotional intelligence on the coaching relationship

The impact of emotional intelligence on the coaching relationship is profound, as it shapes the connection between coach and coachee, enabling deeper and more effective growth. The coaching relationship is unique in that it relies on trust, mutual respect and a shared dedication to the coachee's development. Emotional intelligence is the key factor that makes this dynamic work. It allows coaches to create an environment where coachees feel safe enough to explore their vulnerabilities, challenge their assumptions and take meaningful risks in pursuit of their goals.

The sections that follow describe how emotional intelligence enhances the coaching relationship.

Building trust

Trust is the cornerstone of any successful coaching relationship, and emotional intelligence is what builds that trust. When coachees sense that you're self-aware, empathetic and in control of your emotions, they are more likely to trust you. Trust grows when coaches are consistent in their emotional responses, demonstrate a genuine interest in their coachees' wellbeing and show that they are fully present during coaching conversations. With high emotional intelligence, a coach can tune in to subtle cues that indicate whether the coachee feels understood and valued. This level of attunement builds a strong emotional foundation that fosters deep trust over time.

Fostering open communication

Emotional intelligence enables coaches to communicate in ways that are clear, compassionate and non-judgemental. This creates a space where coachees feel comfortable being vulnerable, expressing doubts and discussing challenges. When coaches demonstrate empathy and understanding, coachees are more likely to open up about the obstacles they are facing – both personal and professional. Emotional intelligence also helps coaches listen beyond the words, picking up on emotional undertones and body language, which can reveal deeper issues that the coachee may not yet be aware of. This empathic listening encourages a more authentic and open dialogue, allowing coachees to be honest not only with the coach but also with themselves.

Navigating conflict

Difficult conversations are an inevitable part of coaching, whether it is addressing a coachee's resistance to change, conflicting values or tough feedback. With emotional intelligence, coaches can approach conflict with calmness and empathy. Instead of reacting defensively, they manage their own emotional responses, enabling them to handle sensitive topics in a way that doesn't escalate tension. Coaches with high emotional intelligence can also depersonalise conflict, focusing on the issue at hand rather than allowing emotions to cloud the conversation. This helps coachees feel supported, even when faced with tough truths, and empowers them to navigate conflicts constructively. Coaches who remain emotionally balanced during these moments model how to handle challenges effectively, which can inspire coachees to develop similar emotional resilience.

Supporting coachee growth

Perhaps one of the most significant ways emotional intelligence impacts the coaching relationship is in the coach's ability to support and facilitate the coachee's growth. When you are attuned to your coachee's emotional state, you can gauge when they're feeling confident and ready to take on new challenges, and when they might be struggling and in need of more support. Emotional intelligence allows you to adjust your approach based on the coachee's emotional cues, offering encouragement, empathy or challenge at the right moments. This responsiveness helps coachees feel supported throughout their journey, ensuring they don't feel overwhelmed or stuck. By recognising when a coachee is in emotional distress or needs additional reinforcement, coaches can provide exactly the kind of support necessary for breakthroughs and sustained progress.

Encouraging self-awareness in coachees

Emotional intelligence encourages greater self-awareness in coachees. Through emotionally intelligent coaching, coachees are prompted to reflect on their emotional triggers, how their emotions influence their decisions and how they can better regulate their emotional responses. As coaches model self-awareness, coachees learn to recognise and articulate their own emotions, which is crucial for personal and professional growth. When coachees develop greater emotional awareness, they are better equipped to navigate challenges, manage stress and build healthier relationships – both within and beyond the coaching relationship.

Deepening empathy and connection

The ability to connect emotionally with a coachee is essential for creating a genuine, human-centred coaching relationship. Emotional intelligence allows coaches to deepen their empathy – not just understanding what a coachee is saying but also truly feeling the emotions they are experiencing. This deep emotional connection helps coachees feel seen and heard on a profound level, fostering a sense of security and belonging within the coaching relationship. When coachees feel emotionally connected, they are more likely to trust the process and commit to their personal development goals. This level of empathy also empowers coaches to offer more tailored, compassionate support that resonates with the coachee's unique emotional journey.

Adapting to individual coachee needs

Every coachee brings a different emotional landscape to the coaching relationship, and emotional intelligence allows coaches to adapt their approach accordingly. Some coachees may be highly self-aware and in tune with their emotions, while others may struggle to articulate or even recognise their feelings. By tuning in to each coachee's emotional state, a coach can tailor their approach – whether that means offering more emotional support, asking reflective questions or providing a safe space for difficult conversations. This adaptability ensures that the coaching relationship is personalised and responsive, leading to more effective outcomes for everyone.

Emotional intelligence is the glue that holds the coaching relationship together, transforming it from a transactional exchange into a powerful, trust-based partnership. It enhances the relationship in countless ways, from building trust and fostering open communication to navigating conflict and supporting coachee growth. Coaches who develop their emotional intelligence are better equipped to handle the complexities of the human experience, enabling them to guide their coachees through both emotional challenges and personal breakthroughs. In this way, emotional intelligence is not just a skill; it is a fundamental quality that makes coaching truly transformative.

Applying emotional intelligence in coaching sessions

Emotional intelligence isn't just something we talk about; it's something we use in every coaching session. From the initial chemistry meeting to ongoing interactions, emotional intelligence shapes how we approach conversations, set goals and support our coachees.

Here are some ways to apply emotional intelligence in your coaching:

Practical strategies

- Active listening: Listen not just with your ears but with your whole presence. Pay attention to what your coachee is saying: words, tone, body language – all of it. This helps you fully understand their emotions and underlying concerns.
- I-statements: Encourage coachees to use I-statements when expressing their emotions. It's a simple tool, but it helps them articulate their feelings in a way that fosters productive, emotionally intelligent conversations. An example of an I-statement might be 'I feel frustrated when deadlines aren't met because it makes me worry about the impact on our team's success.' This statement focuses on the coachee's own feelings and experiences, rather than placing blame or making accusations, which helps to foster a more constructive and emotionally intelligent conversation.
- Emotionally intelligent questioning: Ask open-ended questions that invite coachees to explore their emotions. Questions like, 'How do you feel about this situation?' or 'What emotions are coming up for you right now?' can lead to powerful insights.
- Emotional reframing: Help coachees reframe their emotional experiences in a constructive way. For example, if they're feeling anxious about a new challenge, help them see that anxiety as a sign of growth and a willingness to step out of their comfort zone.
- Mindful pauses: Don't be afraid of silence. Taking mindful pauses during sessions gives both you and your coachee time to process emotions, especially when dealing with intense feelings or complex issues.

The transformative power of emotional intelligence

Emotional intelligence has the power to turn coaching from a simple process into a profound experience of personal growth and self-discovery. For coachees, developing emotional intelligence through coaching can lead to greater self-awareness, improved relationships and better problem-solving skills. For us as coaches, cultivating emotional intelligence is what enables us to create these transformative experiences. When we hone our emotional intelligence, we're better equipped to read the emotional cues of those we are coaching, understanding not just what they're saying, but how they are feeling beneath the surface.

This deep emotional insight allows us to ask the right questions, offer the right support and guide our coachees through their challenges in a way that resonates on a personal level. It is not just about problem-solving; it is about connecting on an emotional level that makes our guidance more impactful. By developing our emotional intelligence, we can foster an environment where coaches feel truly understood and supported, leading to breakthroughs that might not otherwise happen. In essence, our emotional intelligence is the key to unlocking the full potential of our coaching, turning ordinary sessions into powerful, life-changing experiences.

As coachees become more emotionally intelligent, they start seeing themselves and their challenges more clearly. They learn to manage their emotions, communicate more effectively, and make decisions that align with their true values and goals. And the impact doesn't stop there – it ripples out into their personal lives, improving their relationships and overall wellbeing.

Here's what that ripple effect looks like:

- Personal growth: Coachees who develop emotional intelligence often experience significant personal growth. They become more resilient, more confident, and more capable of handling life's ups and downs.
- Improved relationships: With greater empathy and understanding, coachees navigate their relationships more effectively, leading to stronger, more fulfilling connections.
- Enhanced decision-making: With increased self-awareness and emotional regulation, coachees make decisions that are thoughtful and aligned with their long-term goals.

- Empowerment: Ultimately, emotional intelligence empowers coachees to take control of their lives. They learn that while they can't always control external circumstances, they can control how they respond to them.

In conclusion, emotional intelligence is the cornerstone of effective coaching. It's the lens through which we see our coachees, the tool that guides our interactions, and the foundation upon which we build trust and rapport. By cultivating and applying emotional intelligence in our coaching practice, we enhance the coaching relationship and help our coachees achieve deeper, more meaningful transformations. Emotional intelligence isn't just a skill – it's the heart and soul of what makes coaching a truly transformative experience.

Summary

- Coaching relies on emotional intelligence as a foundational element for understanding and managing emotions, both for the coach and the coachee.
- Emotional awareness in coaching creates a safe and supportive environment, allowing for deeper, more meaningful conversations.
- Coaching effectiveness is enhanced by the key components of emotional intelligence, including self-awareness, self-regulation, empathy, social skills and motivation.
- Coaches who cultivate emotional intelligence can build trust, navigate conflicts and support the emotional growth of their coachees.
- Emotional intelligence is applied in coaching through techniques such as active listening, using I-statements, emotionally intelligent questioning, reframing emotions and taking mindful pauses.
- Coaching with a focus on emotional intelligence empowers coachees to achieve personal growth, improve relationships and make decisions aligned with their values.
- Emotional intelligence is positioned as the heart of transformative coaching, driving lasting personal and professional development.

Reflection questions

1. How do my emotional triggers influence my responses during coaching sessions, and how can I become more aware of them?
2. In what ways do I practise empathy with my coachees, and how can I deepen my connection with them?
3. How do I maintain emotional regulation during challenging coaching conversations, and what strategies can I use to stay calm and present?

4. What are some examples of how I've used emotionally intelligent questioning in my coaching practice, and how can I improve this skill?
5. How do I encourage my coachees to explore and reframe their emotions constructively, and what impact has this had on their growth?

Chapter 10
Coaching skills for children and young people

The same principles that make coaching so effective for adults can be incredibly powerful when applied to children and young people. In fact, introducing coaching skills to students at an early age equips them with essential life tools that foster independence, resilience and emotional intelligence.

In this chapter, we will explore how coaching can be adapted to support children and young people in their development. Just as with adults, coaching for young learners encourages reflection, active listening and self-directed growth. It invites them to think more critically about their choices, actions and relationships, empowering them to take ownership of their learning and personal development.

The beauty of coaching for young people lies in its ability to help them develop essential skills, such as communication, problem-solving and self-regulation – skills that will serve them well beyond the classroom. As we have explored the strategies for introducing coaching in educational settings, you will now see how fostering a coaching culture with students creates a space where they feel supported, heard and equipped to navigate the challenges of growing up in today's world.

Understanding the power of coaching for children and young people

Children and young people are constantly learning how to navigate their world, develop relationships and understand themselves. While schools often focus on academic growth, the development of emotional and social skills is just as critical. Coaching for young learners helps bridge that gap. By teaching children how to ask questions, reflect on their experiences and make empowered decisions, coaching gives them tools to build independence and resilience. It shifts the dynamic from being told what to do to discovering what they are capable of on their own.

For example, consider a student who struggles with time management and often finds themself feeling overwhelmed by deadlines. Instead of being told how to structure their time, a coaching session could involve the teacher asking open-ended questions like, 'How do you currently manage your time for homework?' or 'What has worked for you in the past when you've had multiple tasks?' Through reflective questioning, the student might realise that they tend to procrastinate because they feel anxious about starting bigger tasks. Once this insight emerges, the coach could guide them towards exploring strategies they feel comfortable trying, such as breaking assignments into smaller steps or setting a timer for focused work sessions. This approach empowers the student to take ownership of their own problem-solving process. Rather than simply being given instructions, the student learns to reflect on their habits, understand the root of their challenges and develop personalised strategies that fit their needs. As a result, they become more independent and resilient, capable of applying these skills in various contexts both academically and personally.

When young people engage in coaching, they begin to take ownership of their actions, thoughts and feelings. This shift not only empowers them academically but also fosters personal growth. Students like the one in the example above become more self-aware and confident in their ability to manage challenges, both in and out of the classroom.

Building emotional intelligence through coaching

One of the most impactful benefits of coaching for children and young people is the development of emotional intelligence. For young learners, developing these skills early on can have long-term benefits, both academically and personally. Coaching conversations provide a safe and supportive space for students to explore their emotions and learn how to handle them constructively. In coaching sessions, students are encouraged to identify their feelings and consider how those emotions influence their actions. For instance, a student might feel overwhelmed by a difficult maths problem and respond with frustration or avoidance. Rather than being given direct solutions, a coach might ask reflective questions like, 'What are you feeling right now?' or 'How does this frustration affect how you approach the task?' This type of inquiry helps the student slow down and examine their emotional response.

They begin to understand that emotions such as frustration or anxiety are natural reactions but that they can be managed with the right strategies.

As students become more aware of their emotional triggers, they can begin to build resilience. They learn that emotions, while powerful, are not fixed; they can be acknowledged and then addressed in productive ways. For example, a student who identifies frustration as a recurring emotion might work with their coach to develop coping strategies, such as taking deep breaths, breaking tasks into smaller steps or practising positive self-talk. This ability to self-regulate not only helps them tackle immediate challenges but also builds long-term emotional resilience. In addition to understanding their own emotions, coaching helps students develop empathy and better interpersonal skills. When students are more attuned to their feelings, they become more sensitive to the emotions of others. This emotional awareness fosters better communication, and strengthens relationships with peers and teachers. A student who has learned to manage their own frustration, for instance, might be better equipped to support a friend who is experiencing similar feelings, creating a more supportive and connected classroom environment.

Coaching also encourages students to recognise the relationship between emotions and outcomes. By understanding how their emotional state influences their actions – whether it leads to productive effort or avoidance – students gain insight into how to navigate challenges more effectively. Over time, they develop a toolkit of emotional strategies they can apply in various contexts, from tackling academic stress to managing conflicts with peers. These reflective moments help children and young people build emotional awareness, self-regulation and resilience, all of which are crucial for navigating both academic and personal challenges. As emotional intelligence is developed through coaching, students become more capable of handling stress, communicating their needs and understanding the emotions of others. This skill set becomes a vital component of their growth, equipping them to thrive not just in the classroom but in all areas of life.

Fostering independence and problem-solving

At its core, coaching is about encouraging self-directed growth, a concept that is especially powerful when applied to children and young people. Instead of offering solutions or quick fixes, coaching invites students to explore their own problem-solving abilities and develop the critical thinking skills necessary for overcoming challenges. By guiding students with open-ended questions like, 'What do you think could be a good next step?' or 'How have you handled similar situations before?' coaching encourages reflection and independent thought. This process builds a mindset of personal responsibility and empowerment, allowing young learners to become active agents in their own growth.

Rather than relying on external guidance from teachers, parents or peers, coaching helps students shift their focus inwards. It teaches them to assess situations from multiple perspectives, weigh their options, and come up with strategies that suit their unique needs and abilities. For example, a student struggling with an upcoming presentation might be tempted to ask for help writing their speech. Instead, through coaching, they might be encouraged to reflect on past experiences and consider which strategies – such as practising in front of a mirror or breaking the presentation into smaller sections – would help them feel more prepared. By arriving at their own solutions, they not only solve the immediate problem but also strengthen their ability to tackle similar tasks in the future.

This internal exploration fosters independence, enabling young people to develop the confidence and skills to navigate academic, social and emotional challenges on their own. The process of coaching emphasises that mistakes are not failures but opportunities to learn and grow. When students are allowed to experiment with different approaches and reflect on the outcomes, they gain a deeper understanding of what works for them, reinforcing their problem-solving skills and resilience.

As students practise self-directed problem-solving, they become more comfortable making decisions, evaluating consequences and taking responsibility for their actions. These are essential life skills that extend beyond the classroom. The independence nurtured through coaching equips young people to handle personal struggles, peer relationships and important decision-making moments with greater confidence and clarity. Whether they are navigating a difficult friendship, deciding how to manage their time or working through a family conflict, the ability to think critically and independently gives them the tools to make thoughtful, empowered choices. In academic settings, this shift from external guidance to internal exploration changes the dynamic of learning. Students no longer wait passively for answers; instead, they become active participants in their education, curious and engaged in finding solutions. This independence transforms not only their approach to learning but also their sense of self-efficacy – they realise that they have the capability to overcome obstacles and succeed on their own terms.

Ultimately, fostering independence and problem-solving through coaching equips children and young people with lifelong skills. They learn to trust their own judgement, adapt to new situations and take ownership of their growth. This sense of empowerment builds resilience, allowing them to confidently face the complexities of growing up, make informed decisions, and contribute meaningfully to their own development and to their communities.

Promoting positive communication skills

Coaching places a strong emphasis on effective communication, an essential skill for success in both school and life. Through the coaching process, young learners develop the ability to express themselves clearly, listen actively and engage in meaningful conversations – skills that are particularly important during the formative years when students are learning how to navigate friendships, peer dynamics and relationships with adults.

Coaching provides a supportive environment where students can practise communication in a structured, reflective manner. For example, a student who struggles with speaking up in class might work with a coach to explore why they feel hesitant to participate. Through guided questioning, such as, 'What makes you feel unsure about sharing your ideas?' or 'What would help you feel more comfortable speaking up?', the student can begin to identify the underlying fears or challenges. Once those barriers are understood, the coach can help the student develop strategies such as practising responses beforehand or starting by answering simpler questions. As the student becomes more comfortable with these techniques, they gain confidence in their ability to communicate effectively in a classroom setting.

Similarly, coaching can help students improve their listening skills, which are just as important as speaking in fostering positive communication. In peer relationships, misunderstandings often arise when one person feels unheard or misinterpreted. A student might be coached through a situation where a disagreement with a friend has led to tension. Instead of focusing on defending their point of view, the coach might encourage the student to reflect on questions like, 'How do you think your friend is feeling right now?' or 'What could you do to show that you are listening to their concerns?' This shift in focus helps the student practise active listening – acknowledging the other person's feelings and working towards a resolution through empathy and understanding.

One of the most valuable communication skills students learn through coaching is how to resolve conflicts constructively. Imagine a scenario where a student has had a disagreement with a peer during a group project. Rather than avoiding the issue or escalating the conflict, the coach might guide the student in identifying the root of the disagreement and encourage them to use I-statements to express their feelings – such as, 'I felt frustrated when our ideas clashed because I wanted us to collaborate better.' This approach fosters open dialogue while reducing defensiveness, allowing the student to express their emotions in a way that promotes resolution and understanding.

Coaching also helps students become more comfortable asking for help when they need it, which is a critical aspect of communication that many young people find challenging. For instance, a student who is struggling with a difficult subject might feel embarrassed or fearful of seeking help from a teacher. Through coaching, they might explore why they hesitate, and practise how to approach their teacher with a clear, confident request for support – such as, 'I'm finding this topic challenging and I would appreciate some extra guidance to help me understand it better.' This skill not only improves academic performance but also builds confidence in self-advocacy, an important life skill.

In personal relationships, these improved communication skills lead to stronger connections and healthier interactions. As students learn to express their thoughts and feelings more effectively, they build deeper relationships with peers, teachers and adults. They become more adept at handling conflicts, asking for what they need, and participating in meaningful conversations where both sides feel heard and respected.

Ultimately, coaching equips young people with the communication tools they need to succeed in all areas of life. By helping them understand the impact of their words and the power of active listening, coaching fosters a more thoughtful, empathetic approach to interaction. Whether resolving conflicts, collaborating on projects or simply sharing their thoughts, students who have developed strong communication skills through coaching are better prepared to build lasting, positive relationships throughout their lives.

Creating a coaching culture in schools

To fully realise the transformative benefits of coaching for children and young people, schools need to embrace a coaching culture. This goes beyond providing occasional coaching sessions; it requires integrating coaching principles into everyday interactions and classroom practices. Teachers, staff and administrators should be equipped with coaching skills that enable them to model reflective listening, ask open-ended questions, and create an environment where students feel safe to express themselves and explore their ideas.

Establishing a coaching culture transforms the conventional teacher–student hierarchy into a more collaborative and inclusive model of learning. In such a culture, students are not passive recipients of knowledge but are seen as active participants in their own education, capable of making thoughtful contributions to their personal growth and the learning community. This approach encourages autonomy and accountability, empowering students to take ownership of their learning journey. For example, instead of simply delivering instructions or providing answers, a teacher might use coaching techniques like asking, 'What do you think could be another way to approach this problem?' or 'How would you describe your learning experience so far?' These types of questions not only prompt students to think more deeply but also foster a sense of ownership and self-direction in their learning. The goal is to encourage students to reflect, set goals and seek out solutions, all within a supportive framework.

Establishing a coaching culture shifts the traditional teacher–student dynamic into a more collaborative and inclusive approach to learning. In this environment, students are not passive recipients of information but are actively engaged in their own education, contributing meaningfully to their personal growth and the learning community. This approach promotes autonomy and accountability, empowering students to take control of their learning journey. For instance, rather than simply giving instructions or answers, a teacher might ask, 'What do you think could be another way to approach this problem?' or 'How would you describe your learning experience so far?' These types of questions encourage deeper thinking and help students develop ownership and self-direction in their learning. The aim is to support students as they reflect, set goals and find solutions within a nurturing environment.

When schools adopt a coaching mindset, they create an environment where students feel encouraged to explore, reflect and grow. This supportive, respectful setting helps foster resilience, critical thinking and emotional intelligence. A coaching culture doesn't just benefit individual students; it strengthens the entire school community by promoting a sense of shared responsibility for growth. As teachers and staff model these coaching behaviours in their daily interactions, students become more confident, engaged learners who contribute actively to the school's learning environment. Over time, this approach leads to deeper connections among students, teachers and staff, transforming the school into a more dynamic, inclusive and innovative place to learn. By fostering a culture of coaching, schools cultivate an atmosphere where learning is not only about achieving academic goals but also about personal development, collaboration and continuous growth.

This shift fundamentally changes the way education is experienced, making it a more holistic and empowering process for everyone involved.

Long-term benefits of coaching for young people

The long-term benefits of coaching for children and young people extend far beyond the classroom. As they continue to develop emotional intelligence, communication skills and problem-solving abilities through coaching, these young learners are better equipped to face the complexities of adulthood. The skills gained through coaching – such as self-awareness, resilience and independence – become invaluable as they navigate future academic challenges, personal relationships and career decisions. Coaching helps students build a strong foundation of self-awareness, which enables them to recognise their strengths and areas for growth. This self-knowledge is critical when making decisions about their education, career paths or relationships. For example, a student who has developed emotional intelligence through coaching may be better able to manage stress during a university application process or handle conflict in a workplace setting. The ability to regulate emotions, think critically and approach challenges with a problem-solving mindset allows students to handle life's inevitable ups and downs with greater confidence and clarity.

Coaching instils a sense of independence and responsibility that prepares students for life's uncertainties. As young people develop the capacity to reflect on their choices and take ownership of their actions, they become more capable of adapting to new environments and challenges. Whether it is managing the transition to higher education, entering the workforce or building meaningful personal relationships, the skills they gain from coaching provide a solid framework for success. Introducing coaching at an early age also invests in the long-term wellbeing of students. These foundational skills create resilient, reflective and empowered individuals who are better equipped to contribute positively to society. A student who has learned to listen actively, communicate effectively and solve problems independently is more likely to engage productively in their community, collaborate well with others and advocate for positive change. Furthermore, coaching helps to cultivate a mindset of continuous learning and personal growth. As students carry these skills into adulthood, they are more likely to seek out opportunities for self-improvement, take on leadership roles, and approach life with curiosity and a growth-oriented perspective. This long-term approach to personal development ensures that they are not just prepared to succeed academically but are also equipped to lead fulfilling, impactful lives.

In the broader context, the ripple effect of coaching extends to society as a whole. Resilient, emotionally intelligent and self-aware individuals are better positioned to contribute to building healthier communities, workplaces and social systems. As they grow into adults who value collaboration, empathy and reflection, they help shape a world that is more inclusive, adaptable and innovative. By embedding coaching principles early in life, schools are making an investment in the future success and wellbeing of their students, preparing them to face whatever challenges lie ahead with confidence and purpose. The long-term impact of coaching truly goes beyond the individual, contributing to the creation of a more thoughtful, resilient and empowered generation.

Summary

- Coaching has a profound impact on children and young people, equipping them with skills that go beyond academic learning.
- Coaching fosters emotional intelligence, independence, problem-solving abilities and strong communication skills, helping students manage personal, social and academic challenges with confidence.
- Self-directed growth and positive communication are promoted through coaching, preparing young learners for adulthood with resilience, self-awareness and empathy.
- The chapter emphasises the importance of embedding a coaching culture in schools, where students are active participants in their learning and development.
- Coaching shapes students into reflective, empowered individuals who contribute positively to society, with long-term benefits for personal and social growth.

Reflection questions

1. How might coaching techniques enhance your ability to manage challenges in both academic and personal settings?
2. In what ways could improving your emotional intelligence through coaching impact your relationships with peers and your wider network and community?
3. How does developing problem-solving skills through coaching help you take ownership of your decisions and actions?

4. How can active listening and improved communication skills influence your ability to resolve conflicts and collaborate effectively with others?
5. What changes could occur in your learning experience if your school adopted a more collaborative, coaching-based approach to education?

Chapter 11
Coaching skills for parents: empowering families in school communities

Building trust and bridging gaps

Coaching skills for parents is a deeply personal topic for me. Over the past few years, I have seen first-hand how essential these skills are within school communities. Through my experience working and advocating within the neurodiversity space and leading two schools for autistic children and young people, I have witnessed how often families and parents feel excluded from important conversations about their children's development and wellbeing. In many cases, professionals form strong opinions about a child's needs, making decisions in meetings where the parents – who intimately know their child's strengths, challenges and day-to-day realities – are either not consulted or their insights are minimised. This disconnect can leave families feeling stressed, worried and anxious about their child's future, as if decisions are being made about them rather than with them. When parents feel sidelined, it can erode trust and create barriers that limit the potential for positive collaboration.

This exclusion not only creates emotional distress for parents but can also result in a misalignment between the support provided at school and what the child needs at home. Parents often feel they are left navigating complex systems alone, frustrated by the lack of transparency and communication from professionals. The gap between school and home can grow wider as families struggle to understand how decisions are being made and why their voices seem unheard. Over time, this can lead to disengagement, leaving families to feel that their input is undervalued, despite their unique and critical perspective on their child's needs.

Breaking this cycle begins with the coaching skill of giving attention. Simple yet powerful techniques like listening, paraphrasing and summarising can open the door to building trust. When someone truly listens – when parents feel heard and understood – it not only validates their experiences but helps create a collaborative space where mutual understanding can flourish. This is not just a surface-level exchange; it is about creating a connection that encourages parents to speak openly, knowing their insights are respected and considered. Active listening ensures that parents' voices are part of the decision-making process, and that they are seen as equal partners in their child's journey.

The importance of these skills is particularly profound in the field of neurodiversity in the United Kingdom, where navigating the complex landscape of support and provision can be overwhelming for families. From education health care plans (EHCPs) in England to accessing the right therapies or understanding funding options, parents often feel they are left to figure out a fragmented system on their own. Coaching skills such as empathetic listening, reflecting back parents' concerns and encouraging collaborative problem-solving can make an enormous difference in reducing the anxiety and isolation families may feel. These techniques enable parents to feel more engaged, helping them to advocate for their child with confidence and clarity.

Moreover, when schools and professionals adopt a coaching mindset, it changes the dynamic of the parent–professional relationship. Rather than positioning professionals as the sole experts, it encourages an environment of shared expertise, where both parents and professionals contribute to the conversation. This shift in perspective fosters greater collaboration, ensuring that the child's needs are understood in a holistic way, and that the solutions are tailored to both school and home environments. In this way, the bridge between home and school becomes stronger, built on a foundation of trust, mutual respect and shared commitment to the child's success.

Ultimately, coaching skills do more than improve communication – they have the power to transform relationships. When trust is established, it creates a ripple effect, making the entire support network stronger and more effective. Schools become places where parents feel empowered to contribute, professionals feel supported in their work, and children benefit from a more connected and cohesive approach to their education and development. The ability to bridge these gaps, particularly in the neurodiversity space, ensures that families are no longer navigating the system alone but are supported in meaningful, collaborative ways that honour their voice and their child's unique needs.

Practical strategies for building parent partnerships through coaching

Building strong parent partnerships is essential for creating a supportive and successful educational environment for students. These partnerships thrive on trust, open communication and mutual respect. However, fostering such relationships can be challenging when parents feel disconnected from the decision-making process or overwhelmed by the complexities of their child's educational needs. Coaching offers a powerful approach to bridge this gap by focusing on empowering parents and strengthening the connection between families and schools.

Practical strategies for building parent partnerships through coaching emphasise the creation of open, trust-based communication channels where parents feel genuinely heard, respected and engaged. By using coaching techniques like active listening, paraphrasing and asking open-ended questions, educators can move beyond merely informing parents to involving them as equal partners in their child's learning journey. These strategies are not just about improving communication; they are about building relationships that encourage collaboration, shared problem-solving, and a sense of collective responsibility for the child's growth and wellbeing. In this section, we explore how educators can use these coaching techniques to cultivate meaningful partnerships with parents, creating a school culture where every voice is valued and every family feels connected to their child's education. By fostering these collaborative relationships, educators can ensure that parents are not just observers but active participants in shaping their child's future success.

Practical strategies

Active listening and giving attention

- Create regular opportunities for parents to voice their concerns and share their experiences in a non-judgemental environment.
- Set up scheduled one-to-one meetings or group sessions with parents where teachers and staff actively listen without interrupting. Use coaching techniques like paraphrasing and summarising to demonstrate understanding.

Empowering parents through open dialogue

- Shift from making decisions independently to making decisions collaboratively by encouraging open discussions with families.

- At meetings, ask parents questions like, 'What do you think will work best for your child?' or 'What are your priorities in supporting your child's growth?' Include their insights in the decision-making process.
- This inclusive approach ensures that families feel involved, empowered and respected, leading to better-informed decisions that take the whole family's perspective into account.

Building a coaching culture among school staff

- Train teachers and school leaders in basic coaching skills, such as active listening, questioning and reframing, to support more effective conversations with parents.
- Offer professional development workshops where staff learn how to integrate coaching principles into their communication with parents. Include role-playing exercises to practise techniques like using open-ended questions or avoiding assumptions.
- Teachers and staff will be better equipped to support parents through difficult decisions and transitions, reducing misunderstandings and fostering a more positive partnership.

Creating safe, open spaces for parent–teacher conversations

- Establish regular 'coaching-style' conversations with parents where they can share their concerns or aspirations for their child without feeling judged or sidelined.
- During parent–teacher meetings, dedicate part of the conversation to asking parents how they feel about their child's progress and what support they need from the school. Teachers should avoid offering solutions too early and instead allow parents to lead part of the discussion.
- Giving parents the lead in these conversations encourages them to share insights they might otherwise withhold, helping professionals gain a deeper understanding of the child's needs.

Celebrating small wins and offering encouragement

- Recognise and celebrate the progress that both the child and family are making. Acknowledging and celebrating small wins helps to reduce stress and builds confidence for parents, reinforcing their crucial role in their child's development.

- When communicating with parents, focus not only on areas of concern but also highlight achievements and positive changes. For example, send home regular updates that celebrate small victories and offer praise for how parents are contributing to their child's progress.

Peer support networks
- Facilitate peer coaching groups where parents can share experiences, strategies and emotional support with one another.
- Organise informal parent gatherings or support groups that are structured around a coaching model. Encourage parents to ask each other open-ended questions like, 'What strategies have worked well for you?' and 'How can I support you?'
- This peer-led support builds a sense of community among parents, reducing feelings of isolation and providing them with a network of shared wisdom and resources.

Encouraging self-reflection for parents
- Introduce reflective practices for parents to help them better understand their experiences and identify what support they need.
- During meetings or workshops, guide parents through reflective questions such as, 'What's been the most challenging part of supporting your child this year?' or 'What's one small change that has made a big difference in your child's growth?'

Personalised communication plans
- Develop personalised communication plans that meet the specific needs of each family, ensuring that parents feel supported in their preferred way.
- During initial meetings, ask parents how they prefer to communicate (email, phone, in-person meetings) and what level of detail they want in regular updates about their child. Ensure that all communications are framed with empathy and understanding.

Incorporating feedback loops
- Create feedback loops where parents can provide input on how well the school's communication and support strategies are working for them.

- At the end of each term or significant meeting, ask parents for feedback on the communication they've received. Questions like, 'How has our support been working for you?' or 'Is there anything we could improve to make things clearer?' open up constructive dialogue.

Coaching resources for parents
- Provide coaching resources and workshops specifically designed for parents to help them develop key coaching skills they can use at home.
- Offer workshops or online resources that teach parents how to ask open-ended questions, actively listen and help children solve problems independently, with examples to foster supportive family relationships.
- Equipping parents with coaching skills empowers them to take an active role in their child's development, strengthening family relationships and shared responsibility for learning outcomes.

The importance of coaching skills for parents and communities

Coaching skills are essential not only for parents but for the broader school and community as well. These skills empower individuals, fostering confidence and capability in how they raise their children and navigate their roles within the educational system. For parents, coaching encourages self-reflection, allowing them to assess their parenting journey and understand how their behaviours, beliefs and attitudes influence their approach to raising children. This reflective practice is crucial in recognising how deeply rooted belief systems impact parenting choices and interactions with children. By examining these beliefs, parents can gain a greater understanding of how their perspectives shape not only their relationship with their child but also the overall learning environment they create at home.

Coaching techniques, such as reflective questioning, active listening and fostering self-awareness, are valuable tools that can be seamlessly woven into any learning environment. Understanding what conditions are necessary for effective learning – whether in a family setting, a classroom or the broader community – demonstrates how coaching skills can support and enhance the learning process, making it more adaptive and personalised. For parents, these skills are particularly crucial in helping them feel empowered within the school system. Whether they are at the beginning of their child's educational journey or navigating more advanced stages, coaching provides them with the tools to be actively involved in their child's development. These skills give parents a sense of agency, enabling them to better advocate for their child, communicate more effectively with teachers and engage meaningfully in the school community.

As children transition through various phases of life, coaching skills remain relevant, offering ongoing support, guidance and adaptability that continue to benefit families over time. Furthermore, integrating coaching skills into the fabric of school and community interactions creates a more supportive, inclusive and empowered environment for everyone involved. When parents, teachers and staff adopt a coaching mindset, they foster better understanding, more effective communication and stronger relationships. This collaborative approach enhances the overall school culture, making it a place where parents feel confident, teachers feel supported and students are empowered to take ownership of their learning journey.

In essence, the long-term impact of coaching skills extends beyond individual growth, contributing to the wellbeing of the entire community. By embracing coaching principles, we build stronger, more resilient communities where individuals feel heard, understood and equipped to contribute positively to the collective growth and success of both children and the broader educational environment.

Summary

- Coaching skills play a crucial role in supporting parents.
- Skills such as active listening, paraphrasing and summarising help bridge the gap between parents and professionals, ensuring families feel heard, understood and involved in decisions.
- Coaching skills not only empower parents but also teachers, staff and students, enhancing collaboration within schools and communities.
- By fostering better communication and understanding, these skills create a more supportive and inclusive environment.
- The chapter emphasises that coaching benefits everyone involved, contributing to a more empowered and connected community.

Reflection questions

1. How can you incorporate active listening techniques into your daily interactions with parents to ensure they feel heard and valued?

2. In what ways can coaching skills be used to empower parents and help them feel more confident in their roles within the educational system?
3. What strategies can you implement to create a more inclusive dialogue between families and professionals, ensuring that parents are active participants in decisions about their child's education?
4. How can coaching skills be integrated into the school community to support not only parents but also teachers, staff and students in their personal and professional development?
5. Reflect on a recent interaction with a parent or guardian. How could the use of coaching techniques have improved the outcome of that conversation?

Chapter 12
Coaching supervision for teachers who coach

As more schools integrate coaching into their professional development practices, teachers who take on the role of coach require ongoing support to ensure their effectiveness and wellbeing. Coaching supervision – a structured process that provides coaches with space for reflection, feedback and growth – plays a crucial role in maintaining the integrity of the coaching relationship and safeguarding the coach's professional development.

In this chapter, we explore the importance of coaching supervision for teachers who coach. Just as teachers need reflection and feedback to improve their practice in the classroom, coaches need the same level of support to refine their coaching skills, navigate complex coaching situations and ensure they are delivering the highest quality support to their coachees. Supervision provides a safe space for coaches to reflect on their experiences, challenge their assumptions, and receive constructive feedback that helps them grow both personally and professionally.

We will delve into how coaching supervision can help teachers to enhance their coaching skills, manage the emotional and ethical complexities of coaching, and foster their continuous learning and professional growth. By ensuring that teachers who coach have access to high-quality supervision, schools create a culture of reflective practice that strengthens the entire coaching process, benefiting both coaches and the educators they support.

Enhancing coaching skills through supervision

For teachers who are new to coaching or are in the process of refining their coaching abilities, supervision provides an invaluable opportunity for both personal and professional development. Supervision provides more than just feedback; it creates a reflective space where teacher-coaches can critically assess their coaching practice, seek guidance on overcoming challenges and deepen their understanding of coaching techniques. This ongoing support not only builds the teacher-coach's confidence but also ensures that their coaching skills evolve in response to both their own growth and the needs of their coachees.

One of the key factors that contribute to the effectiveness of supervision is the role of a qualified coach supervisor. A supervisor who is professionally trained and experienced in coaching brings a depth of insight that is essential for the teacher-coach's development. With their expertise, a qualified supervisor can offer more than just general advice – they can introduce the teacher-coach to a broad range of coaching methodologies, help them navigate the complexities of coaching relationships, and provide tailored strategies that align with the teacher's style and the specific context in which they coach.

In a supervisory setting, teacher-coaches can discuss their experiences in a safe, confidential environment. Whether they are struggling with asking the right questions, managing emotionally charged conversations or balancing their own emotional responses, a qualified supervisor is there to guide them. The supervisor can provide structured feedback, often through methods like role-playing, reflective exercises and focused discussion on key coaching skills, such as active listening and questioning techniques. A supervisor with a strong coaching background can draw on their own experience to offer practical examples, helping teacher-coaches apply best practices in real-world scenarios.

For instance, a teacher-coach may initially find it challenging to remain fully present when their coachee brings up difficult or emotionally complex issues. In these moments, the supervisor's guidance becomes invaluable. By sharing strategies for emotional regulation, offering insights into how to hold space for coachees and suggesting techniques for deep listening, the supervisor helps the teacher-coach manage these situations with greater confidence and composure. Similarly, if a teacher-coach struggles with formulating questions that drive reflection and self-discovery, the supervisor can introduce advanced questioning techniques that foster deeper thinking and coachee engagement.

The expertise of a qualified coach supervisor also ensures that supervision sessions are structured and purposeful. A well-trained supervisor will not only help the teacher-coach reflect on their past sessions but also set specific goals for their future development. They support the teacher-coach in identifying areas for growth, whether that involves refining communication skills, understanding the nuances of coachee dynamics, or managing coaching ethics and boundaries. This structured approach allows teacher-coaches to continuously develop their coaching practice in a targeted and meaningful way.

Supervision, when led by a qualified supervisor, also helps teacher-coaches develop greater confidence in their role. Through ongoing reflection and feedback, teacher-coaches gain a clearer understanding of their strengths and areas for improvement. They become more self-assured in managing complex coaching scenarios, guiding their coachees through challenges and fostering positive outcomes. Over time, this leads to enhanced coaching practices, where teacher-coaches can respond with flexibility, creativity and a deepened sense of responsibility towards their coachees.

Moreover, a qualified coach supervisor helps teacher-coaches stay connected to professional coaching standards and ethical practices. Supervision becomes a space where teacher-coaches can explore ethical dilemmas, reflect on their own biases and ensure that they are upholding coaching integrity in all their interactions. The supervisor, equipped with both knowledge and experience, acts as a mentor who not only develops the teacher-coach's skills but also reinforces the importance of ethical coaching practices that prioritise the coachee's wellbeing and development.

Managing emotional and ethical complexities

Coaching can often be an emotionally complex process, especially when coaches are working with teachers who may be experiencing high levels of stress or personal challenges. It is not uncommon for a coach to encounter situations where they need to carefully navigate boundaries, avoid taking on the emotional burden of their coachee, or manage their own feelings of empathy and concern.

Supervision provides a critical outlet for coaches to process these emotional dynamics. It allows them to reflect on how their own emotions may be influencing the coaching relationship and ensures that they maintain appropriate boundaries. Moreover, supervision helps coaches develop strategies for managing challenging emotions, both their own and those of their coachees. This reflection can prevent burnout and ensure that the coach remains emotionally resilient and effective.

Additionally, coaching supervision helps teachers who coach to manage the ethical complexities that may arise during their practice. Ethical issues, such as confidentiality, boundaries or conflicts of interest, can emerge in any coaching relationship. Supervision provides a structured forum for discussing these challenges and receiving guidance on how to handle them professionally. Through supervision, teacher-coaches can align their practice with ethical standards and navigate difficult situations with integrity and confidence.

Fostering continuous learning and professional growth

Supervision is not just about addressing immediate challenges; it is also a process that fosters continuous learning and long-term professional growth. For teacher-coaches, supervision provides an opportunity to stay updated on the latest coaching methodologies, deepen their understanding of coaching theories, and reflect on their overall development as a coach. This continuous learning is essential for keeping the coaching practice fresh, relevant and impactful. In many ways, supervision acts as a form of professional development for coaches. It encourages them to reflect not only on their individual coaching sessions but also on their overall growth as a coach. This reflection may involve setting goals for their development, exploring new coaching frameworks or engaging in discussions about current trends in educational coaching. By fostering a mindset of continuous improvement, supervision ensures that teachers who coach are constantly evolving in their practice, staying aligned with best practices and delivering high-quality support to their coachees.

Supervision also helps coaches maintain a reflective mindset, a key element of effective coaching. Just as coaches encourage their coachees to reflect on their practices and growth, supervision encourages the same level of self-reflection in coaches. This recursive process of reflection and learning creates a culture of continuous improvement, which ultimately strengthens the school's coaching programme as a whole.

Strengthening school coaching cultures through supervision

By investing in coaching supervision, schools are not only supporting the individual development of teacher-coaches but also strengthening the overall coaching culture within the school. When a teacher-coach has access to regular, high-quality supervision, they are more likely to feel supported, empowered and confident in their role. This support leads to better coaching outcomes, as coaches are better equipped to guide their coachees through personal and professional growth.

Moreover, the process of supervision reinforces a school-wide culture of reflective practice and continuous development. It creates a feedback loop where coaches are constantly learning and improving, and this culture of reflection spreads throughout the school community. Teachers who benefit from coaching supervision are more likely to model reflective behaviours in their interactions with colleagues and students, contributing to a more thoughtful, open and growth-oriented school environment.

The essential role of supervision for teacher-coaches

Coaching supervision is a vital component of effective coaching practice, particularly for teachers who coach within educational settings. It provides a structured space for reflection, learning and emotional support, ensuring that teacher-coaches maintain both their wellbeing and professional standards. Supervision offers targeted feedback, helps teachers navigate emotional and ethical challenges, and fosters continuous professional growth, ultimately strengthening the entire coaching process.

Having a qualified coach supervisor is crucial to the ongoing development of teacher-coaches. With the guidance of an experienced supervisor, teacher-coaches can refine their skills, address challenges with confidence and adapt to the evolving needs of their coachees. Supervision ensures that coaching remains dynamic, effective and aligned with the highest coaching standards, benefiting both the teacher-coach and their coachees.

As supervision becomes an integral part of a teacher-coach's professional journey, the support of a qualified supervisor not only enhances individual coaching practices but also contributes to a broader culture of coaching excellence within the school environment. The result is a more confident, skilled and reflective teacher-coach, better equipped to foster positive change and build stronger, more impactful relationships with their coachees.

For schools looking to embed coaching as part of their professional development approach, investing in coaching supervision is crucial. It not only enhances the skills and confidence of teacher-coaches but also contributes to the creation of a reflective, collaborative and growth-oriented school culture. Ultimately, coaching supervision ensures that both coaches and coachees thrive, creating a positive ripple effect throughout the school community.

Summary

- Coaching supervision plays a critical role in supporting teachers who coach, providing a structured space for reflection, feedback and professional growth.
- Supervision allows teacher-coaches to reflect on their practice, enhance their skills, and manage the emotional and ethical complexities of coaching relationships.
- Feedback received through supervision helps teacher-coaches build confidence and refine their coaching techniques, ensuring high-quality support for coachees.
- Coaching supervision fosters a culture of continuous learning and reflective practice within schools.
- This process strengthens the overall coaching environment and contributes to a more empowered and effective educational community.

Reflection questions

1. How does coaching supervision help you reflect on and improve your coaching practice?
2. In what ways has supervision helped you navigate the emotional challenges that arise in coaching relationships?
3. How can supervision support you in addressing ethical dilemmas or boundaries that may emerge in your coaching role?
4. What specific coaching skills have you developed through feedback and reflection in supervision, and how have they impacted your effectiveness as a coach?
5. How can participating in coaching supervision contribute to fostering a culture of continuous learning and reflective practice within your school?

Chapter 13
Changes to teaching approaches through coaching: the voices of teachers

When researching this book and speaking with teachers about their experiences with coaching, one recurring theme consistently stood out: the profound shift in their teaching approaches. It wasn't just about adopting new techniques; it was about transforming how they engaged with students, both in classroom discussions and beyond. These reflections capture the essence of how coaching has reshaped their practices, leading to deeper, more intentional teaching.

One teacher highlighted the power of patience, something often overlooked in the fast pace of a busy classroom. She shared, 'Bite your tongue just before you are about to speak and allow for that little bit more from the pupil, because usually, I have found that is when they have that light bulb moment.' This small but impactful shift – giving students extra time to think and respond – often leads to more meaningful engagement and breakthroughs in learning.

Another teacher described a transformation in her listening skills: 'I listen to the students in a different way,' she explained, noting how this change had altered her interactions. 'I notice when I am more patient – like when they are going to answer, and I'll say, "Just take your time, you know it's fine …". The class might be there waiting, but somehow everyone understands.' This patience and attentiveness creates a space where students feel heard and respected, laying the foundation for deeper learning and connection.

A third teacher emphasised the importance of recognising where students are comfortable and where they're not. 'It's about tuning in to their behaviours and understanding their comfort zones,' she explained. This awareness allows teachers to create an environment where students feel safe to express themselves, take risks and stretch their learning without fear of failure.

One teacher reflected on how his role in the classroom had evolved: 'I'm less in a position where I'm the teacher and you're the students, dictating A, B, C and D for you to follow. I notice that it's more of a discussion now.' This shift from a directive, teacher-led approach to a more collaborative dialogue represents the heart of coaching's impact on teaching. It fosters a learning environment where students are active participants in their education, rather than passive receivers of information.

Many teachers noted how coaching empowered students to solve their own problems: 'Getting kids to understand the nature of their problems, sift the low-level issues from the higher-level ones and steer their way to a solution is rewarding. It's quite nice to see them coming up with answers to their own problems rather than me just telling them what to do, which is only a short fix really.' This problem-solving approach nurtures independence and critical thinking in students, helping them to build resilience and take ownership of their learning.

This shift towards student autonomy was observed by another teacher: 'The pupil will go away, find the necessary information, work out problems effectively, and then come back to me when I can be more effective.' This kind of self-directed learning is a key outcome of coaching, where students take responsibility for their learning process. Another teacher remarked, 'I noticed that there was almost less unnecessary dialogue and more actioning, with the pupils leading the conversation with me.' This powerful shift signals a classroom dynamic where students are more engaged, self-reliant and proactive in their learning.

One teacher described how coaching extended beyond the classroom with a peer coaching model in his school, where older students coached younger ones: 'I set up a kind of peer coaching model where sixth years coach fifth years. We've seen some really fantastic communication take place between them.' This peer-to-peer support not only strengthens communication skills but also builds a sense of community, collaboration and mentorship among students.

These stories illustrate how coaching can lead to profound changes in teaching practices, aligning with the belief that effective teaching has a significant influence on student learning. As one teacher pointed out, teachers spend the most time with students, making them uniquely positioned to implement coaching strategies that have a lasting impact. By shifting their approaches – whether through patience, listening, student autonomy or peer mentoring – teachers are able to create classrooms that foster deeper learning, independence and a collaborative spirit. Coaching empowers teachers to refine their practice in ways that not only transform their teaching but also enhance the entire learning experience for their students.

Evolving relationships within the school community

It's not just the classroom dynamics that have changed, coaching has also influenced how teachers interact with the broader school community, including colleagues, parents and students. Teachers described a shift in their approach, saying,

'Rather than just focusing on, "Here is a group of children, this is where we need them to be, how are we going to get them there," I started reflecting on how I can help the children get there and support other practitioners as well'.

This reflects a more holistic approach, where the focus is on supporting both students and colleagues in their growth.

Another emphasised the importance of a non-hierarchical approach, explaining,

'For me, it was really important that it was non-intrusive. It wasn't, "I'm the expert and you're learning from me." It was, "What can I do to help you realise this or develop this?"'

This mindset fosters a culture of mutual respect and shared learning, where everyone's voice is valued.

One teacher talked about creating safer, more meaningful conversations among staff: 'I tried to create processes and build capacity that allowed teachers to have more meaningful and safer conversations about their practice.'

This approach – which he called 'coaching for enhanced professional practice' – underscores the importance of creating a supportive environment where teachers can openly discuss and improve their practices.

Another theme that emerged from my discussion with teachers was the value of seeking out and respecting the voices of others. One teacher explained, 'By talking to people and finding out what they think about their teaching experiences, I better understand them. This, in turn, makes me think about how I can approach people differently and avoid treating everyone the same, which I try not to do.' This kind of empathy and understanding is crucial for building strong, supportive relationships in the school community.

Another teacher shared her commitment to transparency and empowerment in leadership: 'I decided that I would be myself, share decision-making with my team, talk them through the process of how I make decisions, and then teach them how to challenge those decisions – and how to challenge me – without fear.' This approach not only empowers her team but also builds trust and fosters a culture of open communication.

One teacher discussed the heightened self-awareness she brings to formal coaching sessions: 'In one-to-one coaching sessions, I'm very self-aware. I notice that every movement I make, every way I frame a question, influences the session's chemistry and outcome.' This awareness is crucial for effective coaching, where the coach's presence and approach can significantly impact the success of the session.

Another teacher described her team-driven approach to professional development: 'In the first semester of the year, I focused on team-driven development. I would approach the team and ask, "What is it as a team that you really want to develop in your teaching?"' This approach raises teacher autonomy and self-efficacy, highlighting the importance of collective growth and collaboration.

Finally, one teacher reflected on her approach to working with parents: 'With parents, I focus on what's happening now, not what's happened in the past. It's like driving – you look forward rather than constantly looking back.' This forward-thinking approach helps build constructive relationships with parents, focused on supporting the student's current and future needs.

These reflections underscore how coaching has not only enhanced individual professional practice but also strengthened relationships across the school community. By fostering open communication, mutual respect and a focus on collective growth, participants have created more inclusive and supportive environments for students, staff and parents alike.

Summary
- Coaching has significantly transformed the teaching practices of several educators, reshaping their classroom interactions.
- Teachers reflected on how learning coaching skills fostered more patient, student-centred discussions in their classrooms.
- Coaching encouraged a shift from directive teaching to a more collaborative approach, empowering students to take ownership of their learning.
- Teachers noticed improvements in their listening skills, patience, and ability to recognise and respect students' comfort levels.
- Coaching has positively influenced relationships within the broader school community, leading to more collaborative and supportive interactions with colleagues, parents and students.
- The chapter emphasises the profound impact of coaching on both individual teaching practices and the collective school environment.

Reflection questions

1. How has adopting a coaching approach changed the way I interact with my students during classroom discussions?
2. In what ways can I further develop my listening skills to create a more patient and supportive learning environment?
3. How can I continue to shift from a directive teaching style to a more collaborative approach that empowers students to take ownership of their learning?
4. What strategies can I implement to foster more meaningful and supportive relationships with my colleagues, students and parents?
5. How can I apply the insights gained from coaching to enhance my professional development and contribute to a more positive school culture?

Chapter 14
Equality of relationships: transforming school dynamics through coaching

In the world of education, coaching has the power to reshape the learning environment by prioritising the holistic development of students and fostering a sense of empowerment among educators. Unlike traditional teaching methods, which often place the teacher as the sole authority, coaching introduces a more balanced and egalitarian dynamic. In this approach, coaches act as facilitators, helping students and teachers alike to identify their strengths, set personal and academic goals, and navigate challenges with greater independence. This method respects and acknowledges the unique experiences, aspirations and learning styles of each individual, creating a more personalised and engaging educational experience.

The shift from hierarchical to collaborative relationships

One of the most profound impacts of coaching is how it transforms relationships within schools. Traditionally, schools in the United Kingdom operate within a hierarchical structure, where senior leadership teams make decisions and teachers are expected to implement them. However, when coaching becomes embedded in a school's culture, these boundaries begin to blur, allowing for a more collaborative and egalitarian approach. Coaching nurtures an environment where everyone – teachers, students and administrators – is valued as an integral contributor to the school's collective success.

Michael Fullan (2001) highlights this shift as a movement away from the traditional top-down model towards a more participative, inclusive structure. In this coaching-driven environment, professional development becomes a shared responsibility, no longer seen as something imposed by leadership but as a collective effort to enhance practice. Teachers feel more like partners in the educational journey, actively shaping their professional growth and contributing to the school's direction. This sense of agency empowers teachers to take ownership of their development, leading to greater engagement, creativity and investment in school initiatives.

Moreover, this shift extends beyond staff relationships. When teachers are empowered through coaching, they are better equipped to extend that same agency to their students. The principles of coaching – active listening, empathy and fostering autonomy – naturally ripple into classroom dynamics. Students are encouraged to take ownership of their learning, becoming more active participants in their education. This shift creates a learning environment where students, much like the staff, feel heard and valued, driving deeper engagement, stronger relationships and greater academic success.

The transition from hierarchy to collaboration not only flattens the power structure but also fosters a culture of shared responsibility, mutual respect and ongoing dialogue. The traditional barriers between leadership and teaching staff dissolve, creating a school community where all members – leaders, teachers and students – work together towards a common goal. This collective approach enhances the learning environment and contributes to the wellbeing, morale and resilience of everyone involved.

As this culture of coaching matures, it supports continuous improvement, innovation and a stronger sense of belonging across the entire school community. By shifting away from a hierarchical model towards one of collaboration, schools become thriving learning communities where trust, openness and shared vision drive success. This collaborative culture not only benefits academic outcomes but also creates a more supportive, inclusive environment for both staff and students to flourish.

Enhanced interpersonal dynamics

The shift towards equality in relationships fundamentally transforms the interpersonal dynamics within a school, creating an environment that fosters genuine collaboration and mutual respect. When the hierarchy is flattened and relationships become more egalitarian, communication flows in ways that simply aren't possible in a more rigid, top-down structure. Coaching plays a pivotal role in facilitating this transformation, promoting open dialogue and trust – essential components for positive and productive interactions. In a coaching culture, senior leaders, teachers, administrators and support staff engage in conversations as equals, allowing them to address conflicts constructively, share ideas without fear of judgement, and support each other's professional growth in more meaningful, authentic ways.

When people feel that they are on equal footing, they are more likely to speak openly, express their concerns and engage in honest dialogue. This level of openness leads to deeper collaboration, where diverse perspectives can be heard and valued. It also reduces tension, as individuals are less likely to feel isolated or overlooked, and instead feel empowered to contribute to the collective success of the school. As a result, stronger, more trusting relationships form among staff, fostering an atmosphere of psychological safety, where everyone feels comfortable taking risks and challenging ideas.

This sense of equality and shared purpose doesn't just improve daily interactions – it builds a more cohesive and supportive professional community. The culture shifts from one of compliance and routine to one of innovation and purpose, where conversations are about working together to build something meaningful. This collective focus on growth, both individually and as a team, nurtures a sense of belonging and investment in the school's mission.

Ultimately, this transformation creates a ripple effect throughout the entire school community. Teachers who feel valued and supported in turn create learning environments where students feel the same. The relationships between staff, students and parents become more open and collaborative, enhancing the overall wellbeing of the school. The shift towards equality and collaboration becomes the foundation for a thriving school culture, one where every individual is empowered to contribute to a shared vision of success and growth.

Empowerment through voice

One of the most transformative aspects of coaching is its ability to amplify voices that might otherwise be overlooked or unheard. In traditional hierarchical systems, teachers often feel they lack the space or opportunity to express their perspectives or focus on their personal development. This creates a disconnect between staff and leadership, where valuable insights and experiences are lost in the rigid structure. Coaching radically alters this dynamic by providing a dedicated platform where teachers are not only encouraged but also empowered to speak up, share their experiences and prioritise their own growth. It shifts the focus from simply meeting external demands to fostering internal development – not just as professionals but as individuals with distinct challenges, strengths and aspirations.

This empowerment through voice is profoundly powerful. One of the teachers I spoke to when I was researching this book described how coaching allowed them to focus on 'me as the teacher', giving them a sense of ownership over their professional journey. Instead of being passive recipients of policies and decisions, teachers begin to actively shape their own development. This ownership is critical, as it ignites a deeper connection to their work, fostering a heightened sense of responsibility and pride in their role. Teachers who feel heard and supported are more likely to engage in self-reflection, seek innovative solutions and pursue continuous improvement. They feel motivated not only to meet the needs of their students but to challenge themselves and grow beyond the traditional expectations placed upon them.

When teachers are empowered to discuss their experiences, their sense of agency extends beyond personal growth. It creates a ripple effect throughout the school. As they gain confidence in their ability to drive change, they become more proactive in contributing ideas and strategies to improve the school as a whole. The empowerment of individual voices fosters a collective culture of shared leadership, where ideas are freely exchanged and collaboration flourishes. In this environment, no one voice dominates and everyone – from teachers to support staff – feels that their input is valued.

A culture that elevates and listens to its teachers naturally leads to a more inclusive and equitable school community. When teachers feel heard, they pass that same sense of respect and inclusion on to their students, creating a learning environment where every student's voice matters. This, in turn, strengthens the overall health of the school, as the benefits of empowerment filter through every layer of the organisation.

Ultimately, this shift lifts the entire school. When teachers are empowered to use their voice, they contribute to a more vibrant, engaged and dynamic school culture. It becomes a place where everyone, regardless of role or position, feels valued and heard. This kind of culture fosters innovation, trust and a collective commitment to the shared goal of student success and school-wide improvement. Empowerment through voice, therefore, is not merely a benefit of coaching; it is a transformative force that reshapes the very fabric of the school community.

Promotion of mutual respect

Coaching naturally fosters mutual respect, which is essential for cultivating a positive and inclusive school culture. In coaching interactions, the focus on equality and active listening sends a powerful and clear message: everyone's ideas, experiences and contributions are valuable. This mutual respect serves as the cornerstone for a culture where differences are not only acknowledged but celebrated, and collaboration is actively encouraged. Decisions are no longer driven by a few voices at the top but instead reflect the input and wisdom of the entire school community. In this environment, respect is not just an abstract value but a lived experience that shapes how staff interact with one another and how they work together to meet the school's goals.

Rachel Lofthouse (2015) emphasises that when mutual respect is at the heart of school relationships, it fosters an environment where teachers and administrators can work together as equals, creating a space for authentic problem-solving and decision-making. This collaborative atmosphere breaks down traditional hierarchical barriers, empowering all members of the school to contribute meaningfully. It shifts the focus from top-down directives to a more collective, inclusive approach, where every voice is heard and valued. As a result, teachers feel more invested in school decisions, knowing that their insights have the potential to shape meaningful change.

This culture of mutual respect not only strengthens the relationships among staff but also creates the conditions for true innovation. When teachers and administrators feel respected and trusted, they are more willing to take risks, share new ideas and experiment with creative solutions. The absence of rigid hierarchy allows for a freer exchange of ideas, leading to more dynamic and effective approaches to both teaching and leadership. Innovation flourishes in this kind of environment because people are not afraid to voice new perspectives or challenge the status quo. They know their contributions will be met with respect and consideration, not dismissal.

Mutual respect permeates the entire school community, shaping relationships with students and parents as well. When staff model respectful and collaborative relationships, students learn to adopt similar attitudes. A culture rooted in mutual respect fosters empathy, understanding and openness among students, enhancing both their academic and social development. Students, too, begin to see themselves as valued members of the school community, capable of contributing their own unique perspectives. By creating an atmosphere where mutual respect is the norm, schools also become safer and more supportive spaces for everyone. Teachers are less likely to feel isolated or disempowered, and students are more likely to thrive in a nurturing environment. As a result, the entire school community benefits. Trust becomes the foundation of all interactions, and conflicts are more easily resolved when respect for each person's input is prioritised.

In this context, mutual respect is more than just a value to aspire to – it becomes a guiding principle that influences every aspect of the school's functioning. It's a transformative force that strengthens relationships, promotes shared responsibility, and builds a cohesive and inclusive community. When mutual respect is deeply ingrained in the school culture, every member of the school – teachers, administrators, students and parents – feels like an integral part of the whole, contributing to a vibrant, innovative and thriving educational environment.

Supporting organisational change

The benefits of equality in relationships extend far beyond individual interactions; they play a crucial role in driving and sustaining organisational change. Michael Fullan (2001) highlights that strong relationships are at the heart of successful change efforts. In schools, when relationships are grounded in equality and collaboration, the organisation becomes more adaptable, innovative, and capable of implementing new initiatives with greater efficiency and enthusiasm. Coaching serves as a powerful tool in fostering this culture of support, respect and shared responsibility, which is essential for meaningful and long-lasting change.

Coaching enables schools to create a foundation of trust and openness, where everyone – teachers, administrators and support staff – feels valued and empowered to participate in decision-making processes. This sense of ownership over change is critical. When teachers feel included and respected, they are more likely to embrace new initiatives, champion innovative practices and contribute actively to the school's continuous development. Rather than seeing change as something imposed from above, they become collaborators in shaping the future direction of the school. This collective mindset shifts the narrative from resistance to engagement, making change not only possible but sustainable.

In a coaching culture, organisational change is supported by a deep commitment to professional growth and development. Teachers are not just asked to implement changes – they are provided with the tools, time and reflective space to understand the 'why' behind these changes and to align them with their own practice. Coaching encourages critical reflection on current practices and invites educators to think creatively about how they can adapt to new demands while remaining true to their educational philosophy. This approach helps schools avoid the common pitfalls of change fatigue and staff disengagement, as individuals feel genuinely connected to the change process.

Furthermore, the collaborative and egalitarian relationships fostered through coaching create a supportive environment where risks can be taken and failures are seen as opportunities for learning rather than setbacks. In such a culture, staff are more willing to try new approaches and share their experiences openly, knowing they will be met with encouragement rather than criticism. This openness to experimentation is essential for fostering innovation, a key driver of organisational change. It ensures that schools remain responsive and flexible, able to adjust to shifting educational landscapes while continuously improving their practices.

When schools cultivate relationships based on equality, they also create a sense of shared accountability for the success of new initiatives. Teachers are more likely to take personal responsibility for the implementation and outcomes of changes, rather than simply complying with directives. This shared ownership of both the process and the results strengthens the entire organisation's capacity for growth. It transforms change from an individual burden into a collective mission, where everyone is invested in the success of the school's vision.

Lastly, coaching not only supports the initial stages of organisational change but also helps sustain it over time. Often, new initiatives fail because the focus on change diminishes once implementation begins. However, a coaching culture provides ongoing support, reflection and adjustment, ensuring that changes are continuously evaluated and improved. This iterative process of reflection and adaptation, driven by empowered and engaged staff, makes long-term, sustainable change far more achievable.

In conclusion, promoting equality and collaboration within schools is not merely about enhancing interpersonal relationships; it is vital to driving and sustaining organisational change. By fostering a culture where coaching empowers individuals, schools become more resilient, innovative and adept at navigating the complexities of educational change. When everyone feels valued and included, change is no longer perceived as an external demand but embraced as an internal commitment to continuous improvement, making it far more likely to succeed and thrive over the long term.

Ultimately, embedding the principles of equality in relationships through coaching shapes the very fabric of a school's culture. When these egalitarian principles are integrated into coaching practices they permeate the entire school environment, resulting in stronger relationships among staff, better outcomes for students, and a more positive and cohesive atmosphere. Schools that prioritise equality in relationships become not only more effective but also more nurturing places to work and learn. This positive culture becomes self-sustaining as the values of mutual respect, collaboration and empowerment spread throughout the school community.

As teachers experience the transformative benefits of coaching, they model these behaviours in their daily interactions, fostering a culture of continuous learning, shared responsibility, and collective success. In this way, equality in relationships does more than enhance individual experiences – it becomes the driving force behind a thriving, innovative and supportive school environment.

Summary

- Coaching transforms traditional school dynamics by promoting equality in relationships, shifting away from hierarchical structures.
- Coaching fosters a more collaborative and inclusive environment where every voice is valued, and all members, teachers, students and administrators, are seen as equal contributors to the school's success.
- This shift enhances interpersonal relationships and supports organisational change, contributing to a positive school culture.
- Coaching empowers educators by amplifying their voices, encouraging open communication and promoting mutual respect.
- Professional development becomes a shared responsibility, with everyone invested in the collective growth of the school.
- As a result, coaching helps build stronger relationships, drive positive change and cultivate a more supportive and innovative educational environment.

Reflection questions

1. How can I incorporate the principles of equality and collaboration into my daily interactions with colleagues and students?
2. In what ways can coaching help me build stronger, more respectful relationships within my school community?
3. How does the shift from hierarchical to collaborative relationships impact my sense of agency and empowerment as an educator?
4. What steps can I take to ensure that every voice in my classroom or school is heard and valued, regardless of position or experience?
5. How can I use coaching to support and sustain organisational change within my school, fostering a more inclusive and innovative culture?

Chapter 15
Transferable skills: beyond the classroom

This chapter delves into the concept of transferable skills and examines the broader impact of coaching on educators, extending beyond their professional roles into their personal lives. It is fascinating to observe how the skills developed through coaching transcend the classroom and influence various aspects of an individual's life. The teachers I spoke to when I was researching this book frequently emphasised how coaching not only refined their teaching practices but also helped them sharpen essential life skills such as communication, emotional intelligence and self-awareness. These skills are not confined to the school environment; they ripple out into personal relationships, decision-making processes and even self-care routines. By fostering a deeper understanding of themselves and others, the teachers found that coaching enriched their ability to navigate complex situations both in and out of the workplace, contributing to a more balanced, reflective and fulfilling life overall.

Enhanced communication skills

Teachers consistently highlighted improved communication skills as one of the most significant benefits they experienced through coaching. Effective communication is the cornerstone of any successful relationship, whether with students, colleagues or even family members. However, coaching brought a new level of awareness to how teachers communicate – not just in what they say but in how they say it. Subtle elements like tone, word choice and body language became areas of conscious reflection and refinement. These seemingly small adjustments can have a profound impact on how messages are received, understood and acted upon. A simple shift in how something is communicated can dramatically alter the course of a conversation, steering it from potential conflict towards resolution, or from confusion to clarity.

For teachers who refined their communication through coaching, the results were transformative. They found that their ability to engage in more positive and productive dialogues improved not only their professional interactions but also their personal relationships. In the classroom, these enhanced communication skills led to better student-teacher rapport, clearer instructions and a more inclusive learning environment. Teachers were able to create a space where students felt heard and understood, contributing to a more positive atmosphere conducive to learning.

Colleagues, too, benefited from these improvements, as coaching-enabled teachers became more effective collaborators and contributors in team settings. The ability to communicate with clarity, empathy and intention helped strengthen professional relationships, making teamwork more cohesive and efficient. These skills allowed teachers to navigate challenging conversations with colleagues more skilfully, promoting a culture of openness and mutual respect within the school environment.

Beyond the workplace, these enhanced communication skills naturally extended into personal relationships, leading to deeper connections and more open, empathetic conversations with family and friends. Teachers often reflected on how being more mindful of their communication helped resolve misunderstandings and fostered healthier, more supportive relationships at home. Whether it was through more attentive listening or being mindful of how their tone affected a conversation, these small but impactful changes brought greater harmony into their personal lives.

This holistic development underscores that coaching is not just a professional growth tool but a life-enriching experience. It equips individuals with the skills to navigate the complexities of human interaction with greater finesse and emotional intelligence. Through coaching, teachers learn to communicate in a way that not only strengthens their professional roles but also enriches their personal lives, leading to more fulfilling, authentic connections with others.

In short, coaching's impact on communication extends far beyond professional boundaries, enhancing every interaction and relationship that teachers engage in. The awareness of subtle communication dynamics – such as how tone can soften a difficult conversation or how body language can open up a dialogue – becomes a powerful tool, transforming how teachers express themselves and connect with others. Through coaching, communication evolves from a basic skill into an art form that shapes more harmonious, productive and fulfilling interactions in all areas of life.

Refined questioning techniques

Another valuable skill that coaching cultivates is the art of asking better, more purposeful questions. All the teachers I spoke to shared how coaching encouraged them to move beyond surface-level inquiries and adopt more thoughtful, reflective questioning techniques – both with their students and in their own personal growth. This shift in questioning can have a profound effect on classroom dynamics. Instead of sticking to factual or yes/no questions, deeper, open-ended questions invite students to think critically, explore ideas more fully and develop their own reasoning. By prompting students to reflect and engage with content at a higher level, teachers create an environment where learning becomes more interactive and meaningful.

The benefits of refined questioning techniques extend far beyond the classroom. Improved questioning is equally impactful in professional meetings, mentoring sessions and even personal conversations. When teachers learn how to ask the right questions, they not only help others uncover insights but also stimulate more reflective thinking in themselves. In professional settings, this skill can lead to more productive collaborations, as colleagues are encouraged to think more deeply and approach challenges from different angles. Asking questions that promote reflection and critical thought enables teams to explore ideas more comprehensively and come to better solutions, fostering a culture of inquiry and innovation.

In personal conversations, refined questioning techniques create space for more open, honest dialogue. Whether navigating complex emotional situations or simply trying to connect on a deeper level with friends or family, knowing how to ask questions that encourage reflection can enhance relationships and mutual understanding. These questions go beyond surface-level exchanges, helping to uncover underlying concerns, motivations or aspirations, which can lead to richer and more meaningful conversations.

Ultimately, the ability to ask thoughtful, reflective questions is a powerful tool that enhances interactions across all areas of life. Whether in the classroom, at work or in personal settings, asking the right questions can lead to deeper insights, stronger connections and a greater capacity for growth – both for the person asking the questions and for those responding. In this way, coaching equips teachers with a skill that has far-reaching implications, transforming not only how they teach but also how they engage with the world around them.

Increased self-awareness

One of the most personally transformative aspects of coaching is the heightened self-awareness it cultivates. Many of the teachers I spoke to described how coaching helped them gain a clearer understanding of who they are – their strengths, areas for growth and what truly drives them. This deepened self-awareness is a game changer, as it serves as the foundation for making decisions that are not only more informed but also more aligned with one's core values and long-term goals. With a stronger grasp of their own motivations and capabilities, teachers found themselves better equipped to navigate challenges, adjust their behaviour and engage more thoughtfully with others.

This clarity enables teachers to make intentional choices about their professional practice, whether that involves adjusting their teaching style to better suit the needs of their students or identifying areas for personal development. It empowers them to face difficulties with a level of understanding that allows for more thoughtful and strategic responses, rather than reactive decision-making. In the classroom, this means being more attuned to how they interact with students, managing stress with greater composure and responding to feedback more constructively.

However, the impact of increased self-awareness doesn't stop at the professional level. It ripples into personal life, enriching relationships and overall wellbeing. Teachers who have developed a deeper understanding of themselves through coaching often find that they are more mindful in their interactions with friends and family. They become more aware of their emotional triggers, communication habits and the way they respond to different situations. This awareness allows them to foster healthier, more intentional relationships, as they approach conflicts with greater empathy and handle personal challenges with more clarity and resilience.

Moreover, increased self-awareness can lead to a sense of empowerment that extends beyond day-to-day decisions. When teachers fully understand their strengths, values and what truly matters to them, they are more likely to pursue opportunities that align with their personal and professional aspirations. This could mean taking on leadership roles, seeking further professional development, or simply making lifestyle changes that promote balance and fulfilment.

In essence, coaching helps individuals become more reflective, mindful and aligned with their authentic selves. This self-awareness becomes the compass that guides their actions and decisions, both in and out of the classroom. By developing this deeper connection with themselves, teachers not only enhance their own personal growth but also positively influence their professional practice and relationships, leading to a more fulfilling and intentional life overall.

Impact on professional relationships

Coaching significantly enhances the relationships educators build in their professional environments. The teachers I spoke to highlighted how their improved communication, self-awareness and refined questioning techniques positively influenced their interactions with colleagues, students and administrators. These enhanced skills have a ripple effect, fostering more open, respectful and productive conversations across the school community. As teachers become more skilled at expressing themselves clearly, listening actively and engaging thoughtfully with others, their professional relationships deepen, creating an atmosphere of mutual respect and collaboration.

The impact of these improved relationships extends beyond individual interactions. When educators feel heard, valued and supported, a more collaborative and cohesive school culture begins to take shape. This type of environment is essential for both successful teaching and learning. Teachers who are better communicators and more self-aware can connect more meaningfully with their students, leading to improved classroom dynamics, greater student engagement and a stronger sense of belonging. In this way, coaching doesn't just benefit the teacher – it enhances the overall learning experience for students, as they thrive in an environment built on trust and mutual understanding.

Strong professional relationships also extend to interactions with senior leaders. Teachers who have developed these essential skills through coaching can engage more confidently in discussions around decision-making, school policies or professional development. This creates a more open dialogue between staff and leadership, breaking down hierarchical barriers and encouraging a more inclusive, participative approach to school governance. Senior leaders, in turn, benefit from a staff that is not only more engaged but also empowered to offer insights, contribute to problem-solving and support the school's mission in a meaningful way.

Ultimately, the positive relationships cultivated through coaching create a supportive and harmonious school culture, where collaboration is the norm, and everyone is invested in the collective success of the community. Teachers, students, support staff and senior leaders all benefit from this interconnected environment, where strong relationships lay the groundwork for innovation, shared responsibility and continuous improvement. As these relationships flourish, the school becomes a place where everyone feels valued, heard and engaged – a space where both teaching and learning can reach their full potential.

Contribution to a supportive educational environment

Coaching creates a ripple effect – what begins as individual growth spreads throughout the entire educational ecosystem. When teachers become more reflective, better communicators and more self-aware, they contribute to a school culture that is dynamic, supportive and focused on continuous improvement. The skills they develop in coaching are not only personally beneficial but also essential for fostering an environment where everyone is encouraged to grow together. This collaborative atmosphere allows teachers to share best practices, offer and receive constructive feedback, and engage in professional dialogues that push the entire school forward.

A school community where coaching plays a central role becomes a place where teachers feel empowered to experiment, innovate and take ownership of their professional journeys. As they gain confidence and clarity in their roles, they are able to more effectively mentor others, contribute to strategic discussions and engage in leadership opportunities. This collective sense of responsibility and empowerment strengthens the fabric of the school, making it more adaptable to change, and more responsive to the needs of both students and staff.

Moreover, the benefits of coaching extend directly to students. Teachers who have refined their questioning techniques, improved their communication and deepened their self-awareness are better positioned to create more engaging and inclusive learning experiences. They can connect with students on a deeper level, fostering a classroom environment where curiosity, critical thinking and meaningful dialogue thrive. This not only enhances the academic experience but also contributes to the emotional and social wellbeing of students, who feel supported and understood in their learning journey. In this way, coaching serves as a powerful catalyst for holistic personal and professional growth, equipping teachers to thrive in all aspects of their lives. The skills developed through coaching are not confined to specific tasks or challenges – they become essential tools for navigating complex situations, building stronger relationships and contributing to a positive, forward-thinking school culture. By focusing on continuous growth and mutual support, schools that embrace coaching create environments where both educators and students can reach their full potential.

Summary

- Coaching has a profound impact on educators, with skills developed extending beyond the classroom into both professional and personal life.
- Coaching enhances communication, refines questioning techniques and increases self-awareness, all of which are applicable in a wide range of contexts.
- Teachers reported that these transferable skills positively influenced their interactions with students and colleagues, and their personal relationships.
- Coaching fosters a more supportive, collaborative and dynamic educational environment.
- The chapter emphasises how coaching contributes to holistic personal and professional growth for educators.

Reflection questions

1. How can I apply the communication skills I have developed through coaching to improve my interactions in both professional and personal settings?
2. In what ways can refining my questioning techniques help me engage more deeply with my students, colleagues and others in my life?
3. How has coaching increased my self-awareness, and how can I use this awareness to make more intentional decisions in my personal and professional life?
4. Which transferable skills from coaching have had the most significant impact on my teaching practice, and how can I further develop these skills?
5. How can I contribute to fostering a more supportive and collaborative culture in my school by applying the skills I've gained through coaching?

Chapter 16
Next steps: bringing coaching into your practice

When I spoke with teachers about what they wanted from a book on coaching, their responses were clear and direct. They wanted practical tools they could use immediately – ways to truly listen and connect with what someone is saying, techniques to break free from fixed ways of thinking, strategies to help students overcome their fear of failure, and guidance on when and how to use a coaching approach in the classroom. They also expressed interest in ideas for using coaching with younger children, and approaches to be less judgemental and more supportive when helping others.

In response to these needs, I have structured this book around the key aspects of coaching in schools. My core belief has always been that teaching is about far more than delivering content; it is about creating connections, fostering growth and nurturing potential. In the fast-paced, ever-changing environment of a school, it is easy to lose sight of the small yet transformative moments that happen every day. Coaching offers a way to slow down, reflect and be more intentional in how we approach those moments – both for our students and for ourselves.

Throughout this journey, we have explored various coaching tools, techniques and mindsets, all grounded in the real-world experiences of teachers and students. We have seen how coaching can transform not only relationships with students but also the ways teachers collaborate with colleagues, approach their own professional development and navigate the complexities of school life. Coaching is more than a set of techniques; it is a shift in mindset – one that fosters empathy, encourages curiosity, and opens up opportunities for growth and change.

As we come to the end of this book, I would like to tie together some of the key themes that have emerged and share how you might take these insights forward in your own practice. Consider the following next steps:

- Start small: Begin by integrating one or two coaching techniques, such as active listening or asking open-ended questions, into your interactions with students or colleagues. Notice how these small changes can open up deeper conversations and foster more meaningful connections.
- Reflect regularly: Make reflection a regular part of your practice. Take time at the end of the day or week to think about how you engaged with students or colleagues. What worked well? What could you have done differently? Reflection helps you stay grounded and continuously improve your coaching approach.
- Foster growth mindsets: Use coaching strategies to help students and colleagues move away from fixed mindsets. Encourage them to see challenges as opportunities for growth rather than obstacles. This shift can have a profound impact on their confidence and resilience.
- Be patient: Change takes time. Adopting a coaching mindset may not happen overnight, but with persistence and practice you will begin to see the ripple effects in your classroom and beyond.
- Stay curious: Coaching is as much about asking questions as it is about providing solutions. Stay curious about your students' and colleagues' perspectives, and be open to what they can teach you.
- Build a supportive network: Coaching doesn't happen in isolation. Build a network of colleagues who are also interested in coaching, and use this group as a space to exchange ideas, share experiences and provide mutual support.

By taking these steps, you can begin to weave coaching into the fabric of your everyday practice, creating a more intentional, reflective and supportive learning environment. Remember, coaching is not just a tool – it is a way of being. It's about slowing down, tuning in and creating space for growth in every interaction. Whether you are working with students or colleagues, or even reflecting on your own development, coaching opens up new possibilities for connection and change.

In bringing coaching into your practice, you not only enhance your own professional growth, you also create a classroom and school culture where everyone – teachers, students and staff – can thrive. That is the power of coaching: it transforms not just individuals but entire communities, fostering a culture of learning, empathy and growth.

Practical tools you can use right away

From the start, I knew this book needed to offer tools that teachers could pick up and use immediately. I have included coaching models like GROWTH and Clean Language, along with strategies for active listening, powerful questioning and fostering self-awareness. These tools don't require a massive overhaul of your practice – they are designed to slot into what you are already doing.

The first step is often the hardest, so my advice is to start small. Choose one or two techniques that resonate with you and try them out. Don't feel pressured to apply everything at once. Coaching is about progress, not perfection, and small shifts can lead to big changes over time.

Truly listening and connecting

One of the most valuable lessons I have learned from coaching is how to truly listen. Not just hearing words, but really connecting with the person in front of me. It is about listening with empathy, without the need to fix or jump in with advice. I know this can be hard in a busy classroom, but when we take the time to listen – whether it is to a colleague, a student or ourselves – we open the door to deeper connections and more meaningful learning experiences.

As you go forward, I encourage you to bring this mindset of deep listening into your daily practice. It is one of the simplest, yet most powerful, ways to show others that they are seen and heard.

Breaking free from fixed ways of thinking

Fixed mindsets can limit both teachers and students. Throughout this book, we have explored how coaching encourages a shift away from fixed ways of thinking and opens up new possibilities. Reflecting on our own beliefs and assumptions, using coaching questions to challenge rigid thinking, and adopting a curious, open attitude can help us and our students unlock new ways of approaching challenges.

When you encounter moments where you or your students seem stuck, remember that coaching is about helping people find their own solutions. Sometimes, all it takes is the right question at the right time to shift perspective and create a breakthrough.

Helping students overcome the fear of failure

One of the most rewarding aspects of coaching is helping students move past their fear of failure. Fear is a powerful barrier, but when we create a safe, supportive environment, we allow students to see failure not as the end but as a stepping stone to growth. Coaching is a powerful tool for building resilience and helping students embrace challenges.

In your classroom, you can create this environment by encouraging reflection, celebrating small wins and modelling vulnerability. Let your students see that making mistakes is part of the learning process, and use coaching conversations to guide them through their setbacks with compassion.

Coaching in the classroom

One of the biggest questions teachers have is, 'How do I bring coaching into my classroom?' As we have discussed, coaching doesn't have to be formal or rigid. It is a flexible approach that you can integrate into your everyday teaching. Whether it is during one-to-one feedback sessions, class discussions or even brief moments between lessons, coaching offers an opportunity to connect with your students on a deeper level.

It is important to remember that not every moment requires a coaching approach. Part of coaching is knowing when to step back and let the student lead the way. Trust your instincts – you know your students and your classroom better than anyone else.

Coaching younger learners

Coaching is not just for older students. As we have explored, younger children can benefit from coaching too, though the approach might look a little different. With younger learners, coaching can be more playful, more exploratory. It is about creating space for curiosity and allowing children to develop problem-solving skills in a way that feels natural to them.

You do not need to ask perfect questions or expect polished answers. Sometimes, the act of asking a simple, open-ended question can spark a child's imagination in ways you didn't expect. Trust that process and enjoy watching them discover their own solutions.

Less judgement, more support

Finally, one of the core principles of coaching is to be less judgemental and more supportive. This has come up again and again in conversations with teachers – they want to be there for their students without jumping to conclusions or imposing their own views. Coaching helps you step back and create a space where the student can think, reflect and find their own path forward.

As you continue your coaching journey, keep this supportive mindset at the forefront. Whether you're coaching a student, a colleague or yourself, approach the conversation with openness and curiosity. You will be amazed at what can happen when you let go of judgement and focus on truly supporting the other person.

Moving forward

As we wrap up this book, I want to remind you that coaching is not a one-time fix or a set of techniques to check off a list. It's a mindset, a way of being and a practice that deepens over time. There is no rush to master everything at once. Instead, focus on small, consistent actions that align with your values and your goals.

Coaching offers us the chance to slow down, reflect and be more intentional in how we approach the transformative moments that happen every day. Whether it is a quiet conversation with a student, a collaboration with a colleague or a personal moment of reflection, coaching invites us to be present, to listen and to trust in the process of growth.

In the end, coaching is about nurturing potential – not just in our students but in ourselves. So, as you take your next steps, remember that you are not just teaching content. You are creating connections, fostering growth and making a lasting impact, one conversation at a time.

As we conclude this journey, it is evident that coaching holds the potential to transform not only individual teachers but entire school cultures. Teachers themselves can act as powerful agents of change, driving the implementation of coaching within schools. With the increasing popularity of coaching in education, more teachers are gaining access to these valuable skills, leading to broader shifts across their institutions. Whether collaborating with students, colleagues or parents, coaching can break down barriers and foster the trust and support necessary for teachers to thrive.

Your next steps

Now that you've explored the concepts and practices of coaching, it's time to think about how you can apply what you've learned to your own context. Whether in your professional role or personal life, coaching can be a transformative tool. Here are some reflections to guide your next steps:

- In your professional life:

- What will be your first action in integrating coaching into your professional context?
- How will you approach this, and who will you involve in the process?
- Consider the time frame – when and for how long will you commit to this first step?
- In your personal life:
  - How can you apply coaching principles to your personal growth or relationships?
  - What is the first change you will make, and how will you measure its impact?
- Planning your path:
  - What do these next steps look like in detail?
  - How will you track your progress over time?

Stay connected and continue learning

Coaching is a journey, and one of the most rewarding aspects is the opportunity to learn from others and share experiences. I am always eager to hear how others are using coaching skills and what insights they've gained along the way.

Whether you're a seasoned coach or just beginning your coaching journey, I'd love to connect and discuss your experiences, challenges and breakthroughs. You can reach out to me directly at jasminemillercoaching@gmail.com or connect with me on social media via @CoachJasmine on X and @jasminemillercoaching on Instagram. I'm also available on LinkedIn at www.linkedin.com/in/jm-coaching.

For more resources, insights and updates, feel free to visit my website at www.jasminemillercoaching.com, where you'll find a wealth of information, including blogs, newsletters and practical tips on coaching in educational settings. These platforms are designed to create a space for continuous learning, where you can explore new ideas, engage with other professionals and further refine your coaching practice.

Further resources for coaching in education

For those interested in delving deeper into the intersection of coaching and education, there are several fantastic resources to guide you, and I have listed these and add to these regularly on my website: www.jasminemillercoaching.com/news/uyubv001dqz39h38o0fs3lti6k4jyk.

These resources will help you deepen your understanding of coaching, providing ongoing support as you refine your skills and apply them in real-world settings. Continuing your learning is essential to staying dynamic and relevant in the evolving field of education and coaching.

Bibliography

Adams, M. (2012a) Coaching psychology in schools: supporting staff performance and well-being. *Coaching Psychology International*, 5(1), pp. 13–21.

Adams, M. (2012b) Problem-focused coaching in a mainstream primary school: reflections on practice. *The Coaching Psychologist*, 8(1), pp. 27–37.

Adams, M. (2016) *Coaching psychology in schools: enhancing performance, development and wellbeing*. Routledge.

Andrew, G.K. and Whittleworth, K.J. (2009) *OSCAR coaching model: simplifying workplace coaching*. Worth Consulting Ltd.

Andrews, J. and Munro, C. (2018) *Flip the system Australia: what matters in education*. Routledge.

Anthony, D.P. and van Nieuwerburgh, C.J. (2018) A thematic analysis of the experience of educational leaders introducing coaching into schools. *International Journal of Mentoring and Coaching in Education*, 7(4), pp. 343–356.

Archer, M. (1995) *Realist social theory: the morphogenetic approach*. Cambridge University Press.

Atwal, K. (2019) The thinking school – the value of coaching. A research working paper. *CollectivED Working Papers*, 8, May, pp. 11–17. Carnegie School of Education, Leeds Beckett University.

Bakkenes, I., Vermunt, J.D. and Wubbels, T. (2010) Teacher learning in the context of educational innovation: learning activities and learning outcomes of experienced teachers. *Learning and Instruction*, 20(6), pp. 533–548.

Barr, M. and van Nieuwerburgh, C. (2015) Teachers' experiences of an introductory coaching training workshop in Scotland: an interpretative phenomenological analysis. *International Coaching Psychology Review*, 10(2), pp. 190–204.

Bennet, P.N. (2019) Teacher coaching in New Zealand secondary schools: an exploratory study. *International Journal of Mentoring and Coaching in Education*, 8(2), pp. 70–85.

Biesta, G. and Tedder, M. (2006) How is agency possible? Towards an ecological understanding of agency-as-achievement. Working Paper 5. The Learning Lives Project.

Biesta, G. and Tedder, M. (2007) Agency and learning in the lifecourse: towards an ecological perspective. *Studies in the Education of Adults*, 39, pp. 132–149.

Biesta, G., Priestley, M. and Robinson, S. (2015) The role of beliefs in teacher agency. *Teachers and Teaching*, 21(6), pp. 624–640.

Birkeland, S., Lemons, R.W. and Stevenson, I. (2015) Improving schools one conversation at a time. *Improving Schools from Within*, 10(20).

Bourdieu, P. (1977) *Outline of a theory of practice.* Cambridge University Press.

Boyatzis, R.E., Smith, M.L. and Beveridge, A.J. (2013) Coaching with compassion: inspiring health, well-being, and development in organizations. *Journal of Applied Behavioral Science*, 49(2), pp. 153–178.

Braun, V. and Clarke, V. (2006) Using thematic analysis in psychology. *Qualitative Research in Psychology*, 3(2), pp. 77–101.

Braun, V. and Clarke, V. (2013) *Successful qualitative research: a practical guide for beginners.* SAGE.

British Educational Research Association (BERA) (2018) *Ethical guidelines for educational research, fourth edition (2018).* Available at: http://www.bera.ac.uk/researchers-resources/publications/ethical-guidelines-for-educational-research-2018

Brock, V.G. (2014) *Sourcebook of coaching history*, 2nd edn. Self-published.

Brooks, R. and Goldstein, S. (2001) *Raising resilient children.* McGraw-Hill.

Brown, C.S. (2011) Implementing preschool curriculum: mentoring and coaching as key components to teacher professional development. *Dissertation Abstracts International Section A: Humanities and Social Sciences*, 71(10-A), p. 3523.

Cantor, S. and Hick, W. (2013) Dialogic OD in practice: conversational approaches to change in a UK primary school. *OD Practitioner*, 45(1), pp. 5–10.

Centre for the Use of Research and Evidence in Education (CUREE) (2005) *Mentoring and coaching CPD capacity building project (2004–2005): national framework for mentoring and coaching.* CUREE.

Chaplin, S. (2007) A model of student success: coaching students to develop critical thinking skills in introductory biology courses. *International Journal for the Scholarship of Teaching and Learning*, 1(2), Article 10.Corrie, C. (2009) *Becoming emotionally intelligent*, 2nd edn. Bloomsbury.

Day, C., Harris, A., Hadfield, M., Tolley, H. and Breseford, J. (2000) *Leading schools in times of change.* Open University.

Doherty, T.L. and Horne, T. (2002) *Managing public services – implementing changes: a thoughtful approach*. Routledge.

Drucker, P.F. (1998) *Peter Drucker on the profession of management*. Harvard Business School Press.

Edwards, A. (2007) Relational agency in professional practice: a CHAT analysis. *Action: An International Journal of Human Activity Theory*, 1, pp. 1–17.

Egan, G. (2002) *The skilled helper: a problem-management and opportunity-development approach to helping*, 7th edn. Brooks/Cole Publishing Co.

Elias, N. (2000) *The civilizing process. Sociogenetic and psychogenetic investigations*, rev. edn. Blackwell.

Emirbayer, M. and Mische, A. (1998) What is agency? *American Journal of Sociology*, 103, pp. 962–1023.

Floden, R.E. and Clark, C.M. (1988) Preparing teachers for uncertainty. *Teachers College Record*, 89, pp. 505–524.

Fullan, M. (2001) *Leading in a culture of change*. Jossey-Bass.

Fullan, M. (2007) *The new meaning of educational change*, 4th edn. Routledge.

Gallwey, T. (1974) *The inner game of tennis*. Random House.

Giddens, A. (1984) *The constitution of society: outline of the theory of structuration*. Polity Press.

Gilbert, M. and Whittleworth, K. (2009) *Coaching supervision at its BEST: helping coaches to coach*. Worth Consulting Ltd.

Gore, M. (2014) The implementation of coaching to enhance the classroom practice of staff in teaching pupils with autism in a generic special school. *Good Autism Practice*, 15(1), pp. 14–21.

Gormley, H. and van Nieuwerburgh, C. (2014) Developing coaching cultures: a review of literature. *Coaching: An International Journal of Theory, Research and Practice*, 7(2), pp. 90–101.

Greeno, J.G. (2006) Authoritative, accountable positioning and connected, general knowing: progressive themes in understanding transfer. *Journal of Learning Sciences*, 15, pp. 537–547.

Griffin, J. and Tyrrell, I. (2015) *Human givens. The new approach to emotional health and clear thinking*. HG Publishing.

Growth Coaching International (xxx) The GROWTH model.

Hawkins, P. (2012) *Creating a coaching culture: developing a coaching strategy for your organization*. Open University Press.

Helsing, D. (2007) Regarding uncertainty in teachers and teaching. *Teaching and Teacher Education*, 23, pp. 1317–1333.

Hollis, M. (1994) *The philosophy of social science: an introduction*. Cambridge University Press.

Hooker, T. (2014) The benefits of peer coaching as a support system for early childhood education students. *International Journal of Evidence Based Coaching and Mentoring*, 12(1), pp. 109–122.

International Coaching Federation (ICF) (2024) *Core competencies*. Available at: https://coachingfederation.org/credentials-and-standards/core-competencies

Jewett, P. and MacPhee, D. (2012) Adding collaborative peer coaching to our teaching identities. *The Reading Teacher*, 66(2), pp. 105–110.

Kamal, K. (2018) Education in the United Arab Emirates. *World Education News + Reviews*. Available at: https://wenr.wes.org/2018/08/education-in-the-united-arab-emirates

Kidd, W. (2009) Peer coaching and mentoring to improve teaching and learning. *Practical Research for Education*, 42, pp. 50–55.

Kline, N. (1999) *Time to think: listening to ignite the human mind*. Ward Lock.

Kline, N. (2009) *Time to think: listening to ignite the human mind*. Cassell Illustrated.

Knight, J. (2006) Instructional coaching: eight factors for realizing better classroom teaching. *The School Administrator*, 63(4), pp. 36–40.

Knight, J. (2007) *Instructional coaching: a partnership approach to improving instruction*. Corwin Press.

Knight, J. (2018) *The impact cycle: what instructional coaches should do to foster powerful improvements in teaching*. Corwin Press.

Kübler-Ross, E. (1997) *On death and dying*. Scribner.

Labaree, D.F. (2000) On the nature of teaching and teacher education: difficult practices that look easy. *Journal of Teacher Education*, 51, pp. 228–233.

Lasky, S. (2005) A sociocultural approach to understanding teacher identity, agency, and professional vulnerability in a context of secondary school reform. *Teaching and Teacher Education*, 21, pp. 899–916.

Leithwood, K., Harris, A. and Hopkins, D. (2008) Seven strong claims about successful school leadership. *School Leadership & Management*, 28(1), pp. 27–42.

Lipponen, L. and Kumpulainen, K. (2011) Acting as accountable authors: creating interactional spaces for agency work in teacher education. *Teaching and Teacher Education*, 27, pp. 812–819.

Lofthouse, R. (2015) *Beyond mentoring; peer coaching by and for teachers. Can it live up to its promise?* Available at: https://www.bera.ac.uk/blog/beyond-mentoring-peer-coaching-by-and-for-teachers-can-it-live-up-to-its-promise

Lofthouse, R. (2016) *Teacher coaching: a collection of think-pieces about professional development and leadership through teacher coaching.* Newcastle University, Research Centre for Learning and Teaching.

Lofthouse, R. (2018a) Coaching in education: a professional development process in formation. *Professional Development in Education*, 45(1), pp. 33–45.

Lofthouse, R. (2018b) Re-imagining mentoring as a dynamic hub in the transformation of initial teacher education: The role of mentors and teacher educators. *International Journal of Mentoring and Coaching in Education*, 7(4), pp. 309–322.

Lofthouse, R. (2018c) Supporting children's speech and language development through inter-professional coaching: a case study of collaboration. *CollectivED Working Papers*, 3, April.

Lofthouse, R. (2019a) Coaching in education: a professional development process in formation. *Professional Development in Education*, 45(1), pp. 33–45.

Lofthouse, R. (2019b) Gathering an international perspective on supporting teacher learning through mentoring and coaching. A CollectivED Symposium summary. *CollectivED Working Papers*, 7, pp. 9–13. Carnegie School of Education, Leeds Beckett University.

Lofthouse, R. and Bulmer, E. (2016) *Teacher peer coaching; a story of trust, agency and enablers.* Available at: https://www.bera.ac.uk/blog/teacher-peer-coaching-a-story-of-trust-agency-and-enablers

Lofthouse, R. and Hall, E. (2014) Developing practices in teachers' professional dialogue in England: using Coaching Dimensions as an epistemic tool. *Professional Development in Education*, 40(5), pp. 758–778.

Lofthouse, R. and Whiteside, R. (2020) *Sustaining a vital profession: a research report into the impact of leadership coaching in schools.* Carnegie School of

Education, Leeds Beckett University. Available at: https://www.leedsbeckett.ac.uk/carnegie-school-of-education/research/collectived/-/media/files/schools/school-of-education/sustaining-a-vital-profession--final-report.pdf

Lofthouse, R., Leat, D., Towler, C., Hall, E. and Cummings, C. (2011) *Coaching for teaching and learning: a practical guide for schools.* Guidance report. CfBT Education Trust & National College.

Lu, H. (2010) Research on peer coaching in preservice teacher education: a review of literature. *Teacher and Teacher Education*, 26(4), pp. 748–753.

Lunenberg, M., Ponte, P. and Van de Ven, P.H. (2007) Why shouldn't teachers and teacher educators conduct research on their own practices? An epistemological exploration. *European Educational Research Journal*, 6, pp. 13–24.

Maslow, A.H. (1943) A theory of human motivation. *Psychological Review*, 50, pp. 370–396.

Munthe, E. (2001) Professional uncertainty/certainty: how (un)certain are teachers, what are they (un)certain about, and how is (un)certainty related to age, experience, gender, qualifications and school type? *European Journal of Teacher Education*, 24, pp. 801–813.

Neale, S., Spencer-Arnell, L. and Wilson, L. (2009) *Emotional intelligence coaching: improving performance for leaders, coaches, and the individual.* Kogan Page.

Netolicky, D.M. (2016) Coaching for professional growth in one Australian school: 'oil in water'. *International Journal of Mentoring and Coaching in Education*, 5(1), pp. 66–86.

Netolicky, D.M., Andrews, J. and Paterson, C. (2019) *Flip the system Australia: what matters most in education.* Routledge.

Pantic, N. (2015) A model for study of teacher agency for social justice. *Teachers and Teaching*, 21(6), pp. 759–778.

Paris, C. and Lung, P. (2008) Agency and child-centered practices in novice teachers: autonomy, efficacy, intentionality, and reflectivity. *Journal of Early Childhood Teacher Education*, 29, pp. 253–268. Preston, T. (2009) *Coach yourself to success.* Management Books.

Priestley, M. (2015) *Teacher agency: what is it and why does it matter?* Available at https://www.bera.ac.uk/blog/teacher-agency-what-is-it-and-why-does-it-matter

Priestley, M., Biesta, G. and Robinson, S. (2015) *Teacher agency: an ecological approach.* Bloomsbury.

Pyhältö, K., Pietarinen, J. and Soini, T. (2012) Do comprehensive school teachers perceive themselves as active professional agents in school reforms? *Journal of Educational Change*, 13, pp. 95–116.

Reinke, W., Stormont, M., Herman, K. and Newcomer, L. (2014) Using coaching to support teacher implementation of classroom-based interventions. *Journal of Behavioral Education*, 23(1), pp. 150–167.

Robinson, V. (2011) *Student-centered leadership.* Jossey-Bass.

Robinson, V. (2018) *Reduce change to increase improvement.* Corwin Impact Leadership Series. Corwin – A SAGE Publishing Company.

Rogers, C.R. (1961) *On becoming a person: a therapist's view of psychotherapy.* Houghton Mifflin.

Scott, S. (2002) *Fierce conversations. Achieving success in work and in life, one conversation at a time.* Piatkus.

Sloan, K. (2006) Teacher identity and agency in school worlds: beyond the all-good/all-bad discourse on accountability-explicit curriculum policies. *Curriculum Inquiry*, 36, pp. 119–152.

Spiegel, J.S. (2012) Open-mindedness and intellectual humility. *Theory and Research in Education*, 10(1), pp. 27–38.

Stillman, J. and Anderson, L. (2015) From accommodation to appropriation: teaching, identity, and authorship in a tightly coupled policy context. *Teacher and Teaching*, 21(6), pp. 720–744.

Timperley, H.S., Wilson, A., Barrar, H. and Fung, I. (2007) *Teacher professional learning and development: best evidence synthesis iteration.* Ministry of Education, Wellington, New Zealand. Available at: https://www.educationcounts.govt.nz/publications/series/2515/15341

Toom, A., Kynäslahti, H., Krokfors, L., Jyrhämä, R., Byman, R., Stenberg, K., Maaranen, K. and Kansanen, P. (2010) Experiences of a research-based approach to teacher education: suggestions for future policies. *European Journal of Education*, 45, pp. 331–344.

Toom, A., Pyhältö, K. and O'Connell Rust, F. (2015) Teachers' professional agency in contradictory times. *Teachers and Teaching*, 21(6), pp. 615–623.

Trautwein, B. and Ammerman, S. (2010) From pedagogy to practice: mentoring and reciprocal peer coaching for preservice teachers. *The Volta Review*, 110(2), pp. 191-206.

Turnbull, M. (2005) Student teacher professional agency in the practicum. *Asia-Pacific Journal of Teacher Education*, 33, pp. 195-208.

van der Heijden, H.R.M.A., Geldens, J.J.M., Beijaard, D. and Popeijus, H.L. (2015) Characteristics of teachers and change agents. *Teachers and Teaching, Theory and Practice*, 21(6), pp. 681-699.

van Nieuwerburgh, C. (ed.) (2012) *Coaching in education: getting better results for students, educators and parents*. Karnac.

van Nieuwerburgh, C. (2014) *An introduction to coaching skills: a practical guide*. SAGE.

van Nieuwerburgh, C. (2017) *An introduction to coaching skills: a practical guide*, 2nd edn. SAGE.

van Nieuwerburgh, C. (2020) *An introduction to coaching skills: a practical guide*, 3rd edn. SAGE.

van Nieuwerburgh, C. and Tong, C. (2013) Exploring the benefits of being a student coach in educational settings: a mixed-methods study. *Coaching: An International Journal of Theory, Research and Practice*, 6(1), pp. 5-24.

van Nieuwerburgh, C., Knight, J. and Campbell, J. (2019) Coaching: a global study of successful practices. *Professional Coaching: Principles and Practice*, pp. 123-140.

van Nieuwerburgh, C., Barr, M., Munro, C., Noon, H. and Arifin, D. (2020) Experiences of aspiring school principals receiving coaching as part of a leadership development programme. *International Journal of Mentoring and Coaching in Education*, 9(3), pp. 291-306.

Vongalis-Macrow, A. (2007) I, teacher: re-territorialization of teachers' multi-faceted agency in globalized education. *British Journal of Sociology of Education*, 28(4), pp. 425-439.

Watts, G. and Morgan, K. (2015) *The coach's casebook. Mastering the twelve traits that trap us*. Inspect & Adapt Ltd.

Whitmore, J. (2009) *Coaching for performance: GROWing human potential and purpose – the principles and practice of coaching and leadership*. Nicholas Brealey.

Whitmore, J. (2017) *Coaching for performance. The principles and practice of coaching and leadership.* Nicholas Brealey.

Willig, C. (2008) *Introducing qualitative methods in psychology.* Open University Press.

Wildflower, L. (2013) *The hidden history of coaching.* Open University Press.

Zeichner, K. and Conklin, H.G. (2005) Teacher education programs. In M. Cochran-Smith and K. Zeichner (eds), *Studying teacher education: the report of the AERA panel on research and teacher education*, pp. 645–736. Lawrence Erlbaum Associates.

Zepeda, S.J., Parylo, O. and Ilgan, A. (2013) Teacher peer coaching in American and Turkish schools. *International Journal of Mentoring and Coaching in Education*, 2(1), pp. 64–82.

Zeus, P. and Skiffington, S. (2002) *The coaching at work toolkit: a complete guide to techniques and practices.* McGraw-Hill.

Zimmerman, J. (2006) Why some teachers resist change and what principals can do about it. *National Association of Secondary Schools Principals Association Bulletin*, 90(3), pp. 238–249.